The Whole Wide World

The Whole Wide World

Placing solutions to poverty into the hands of children

Phil and Rachel Bowyer

Authentic

Copyright 2006 Phil and Rachel Bowyer

12 11 10 09 08 07 06   7 6 5 4 3 2 1

First published 2006 by Authentic Media
9 Holdom Avenue, Bletchley, Milton Keynes, Bucks, MK1 1QR, UK
and 129 Mobilization Drive, Waynesboro, GA 30830-4575, USA
www.authenticmedia.co.uk
Authentic Media is a division of Send the Light Ltd.,
a company limited by guarantee (registered charity no. 270162)

The right of Phil and Rachel Bowyer to be identified as the authors of this
work have been asserted by them in accordance with
the Copyright, Designs and Patents Act 1988

All rights reserved. No part of this publication may be reproduced,
stored in a retrieval system, or transmitted in any form or
by any means, electronic, mechanical, photocopying, recording or
otherwise, without the prior permission of the publisher or a licence
permitting restricted copying. In the UK such licences are issued by the
Copyright Licensing Agency,
90 Tottenham Court Road, London, W1P 9HE

British Library Cataloguing in Publication Data

A catalogue record for this book is available from the British Library

ISBN 1-85078-657-7

Illustrations by Andy Baldwin and Phil Bowyer
Cover design by fourninezero design.
Typeset by Temple Design, Manchester
Print Management by Adare Carwin
Printed by J.H. Haynes & Co., Sparkford

Contents

Contributors		7
How to Use this Resource Effectively		8
The CD-ROM		11
The Poster Pack		12
Introduction	Habits of a lifetime	13
Issues	1. Water and Sanitation	19
	2. Weather and Energy	42
	3. Food	64
	4. Shopping for Clothes	87
	5. Shopping for Food	107
	6. Education	127
Conclusion	Small beginnings	150
Going Deeper	Further information	155
Glossary		162

TO ZACH

...because without you this book would never have happened. Thanks for putting up with Mummy and Daddy as they waded through endless pieces of paper and pictures, and spent hours at the 'puter'. Thanks for allowing us to test out some of our ideas on you. Thanks for testing some of your ideas on us!

Most of all, thanks for your endless questioning about God, the world and everything we take for granted – all of which led us to think that a book like this might be a good idea.

Contributors

We would both like to thank all those who have been influential in growing our awareness of our responsibility to the world in which we live.

Thanks to those people who have contributed specific content to the various materials throughout this resource: Andy Baldwin, Craig Borlase, Mike Hollow, Tim Hughes, Christine Kilipamwambu, Matt Lomax, Furahini Mbwilo, Halima Msiyura, Steve Perry, Richard Smith, Esther Stansfield and David Westlake.

For all your helpful comments, guidance and expertise, thanks to: James Alexander, Mark Arcedeckne-Butler, Nick Burn, Paul Cook, Tara Devlin, Lorna Duddy, John Eames, Keith Etherington, Anna Foxley, Joanne Green, Mari Griffith, Zoe Hayes, Dewi Hughes, Joao Martinez, Rachel Roach, Naomi Sosa, Anthony Titley, Sarah La Trobe, Clare Whittaker and Phil's nan.

In addition, Phil would personally like to thank Tim and Rachel Hughes, Christine Kilipamwambu, Jim Loring, Lindsey Steger and Angelo for your parts in the various mountaintop experiences we enjoyed whilst together in Tanzania.

How to Use this Resource Effectively

What has been done for you
This is a resource designed for families with children aged 4-11. Whether we're parents, grandparents, carers or children's workers, we all have a responsibility to share how God feels about the world we live in with the children we live or work with.

Each chapter is made up of seven family devotions designed to enable children to understand key issues relating to the poor. There are three basic elements:

1. What children might do or say
Everyday situations that children might face, or conversations that you might have with them, that you can use as stimulus or way in to the subject in question.

2. What you ought to know
Provides the parent, grandparent or carer with background information to put the issue in context. This is a crucial element, as it will help you to understand the issues you are going to be exploring with your child/ren.

3. What your family could do
A variety of activities to enable the family to connect with the issue. Naturally, it's down to you how many of these activities you choose to do. We learn by doing, so these activities are often practical. It is important that all family members are involved in the activities you choose to do, not just the child/ren – as it is about learning together and learning from one another. While these activities will be useful to introduce the issues, they may go on to form the basis of lifestyle habits at a later date.

What else has been done for you

CD-ROM
The CD-ROM contains a range of resources to accompany the devotions. These include printables, videos and photographs. They are referenced using the type of resource they are (printable, video, etc.), a number and the title of the resource. For example, the first resource in chapter 1 is called *Printable 1: Buckets*.

Poster Pack
A range of high quality photographs, in the form of a pack, is available direct from Tearfund – and it's FREE. Order yours by emailing enquiry@tearfund.org or calling 0845 355 8355 (ROI: +44 845 355 8355) and quoting order number 16759 and *The Whole Wide World*. It also includes:

- a map of the world
- an education-based board game.

What God can do

The Whole Wide World is all about changing children's and family attitudes and behaviour towards the poor. Your responsibility is to bring your child/ren into contact with God and his values. That's why you share your life with them and teach them what God has said in the Bible. It is then the job of the Holy Spirit to encourage people to see whether there is a need to change.

So be confident:

- in God
- in the Bible
- in the material.

Remember to:

- pray for the child/ren you live or work with
- pray that God will help you to change
- think of ways to help the child/ren to respond to what they have learnt.

What else you can do

- **Extra research**: before you engage in a devotion you could do some extra research. Try websites to get some additional up-to-date info on the subject.
- **Visuals**: think of some visuals that would be useful to set the scene. These could be pictures or objects that you could collect beforehand. Your FREE poster pack will be particularly helpful here.
- **Your own lives**: think about how you can bring your own and your child/ren's experiences into what you are thinking about.

The CD-ROM

Water and Sanitation	Printable 1: Buckets
	Printable 2: 'Spend a penny' label
	Photographs 1 and 2
Weather and Energy	Printable 3: Modes of transport
	Photographs 3, 4 and 5
Food	Printable 4: Oxen pictures
	Printable 5: Money Ox
	Photograph 6
Shopping for Clothes	Printable 6: Washing instructions
	Printable 7: T-shirts
	Interactive 1: Clothes calculator
	Video 1: Lift the Label
	Photograph 7
Shopping for Food	Printable 8: Food and drink
	Printable 9: Fairtrade Mark
	Photographs 8 and 9
Education	Printable 10: Timetable
	Printable 11: Body parts game
	Video 2: My Whole Day
	Photographs 10, 11 and 12

The Poster Pack

Children love to talk about what they see, which is why as part of this resource we have produced a range of high quality photographs, in the form of a pack, which are designed to stimulate discussion, prayer and action. *The Whole Wide World* Poster Pack is available direct from Tearfund – and it's FREE. Also included is:

- a map of the world, which you will need for various activities
- a game to use in the chapter on education.

If you have not already received your Poster Pack, order yours today by simply emailing enquiry@tearfund.org or calling 0845 355 8355 (ROI: +44 845 355 8355) and quoting order number 16759 and *The Whole Wide World*.

Introduction

'If you want to enter life, obey the commandments.'
(Mt. 19:17).

Habits of a lifetime

Half full or half empty?

Seeing things positively in a world with so much poverty is essential. Whether you're a parent, grandparent or someone who works with or cares for children, you'll be well aware of the need to stay positive when it comes to encouraging them. You know that asking a child to 'hold your drink sensibly' is much more likely to have the desired effect than a statement like 'don't spill that drink!' – even though they're saying the same thing.

Seeing the endless opportunities you have to positively impact the poor is far more positive than focusing on the different problems that often seem endless. That way, as you begin to look at the wide range of issues affecting God's world, you'll be better placed to start to consider the responses he's calling you to take in order to begin to help him make it whole again. Perhaps life in general would look a lot different if we focused on what is possible through God, with each other and for others. As we strive to live out God's Word there's sometimes a danger of spending so much time trying to avoid all the things we think we shouldn't do that we never get around to doing the things we know we should do. In reality the Bible is full of positive directions on how to live, and many of these concern how we relate to the poor. God calls his people to do everything in his power to bring justice through everyday actions.

There's a wonderful account in Matthew 19:16–30 of an encounter Jesus has with a man who wants to know what he must do to get eternal life. Jesus' answer is simple: to obey God. The man is sure he's been doing that, i.e. not committing murder, adultery, etc., but he can't help wondering whether he's still lacking something. The problem seems to be that although he's kept all the commandments, in focusing on the do not's, he seems to have neglected some of the do's: 'If you want to be perfect, go, sell your possessions and give to the poor, and you will have treasure in heaven. Then come, follow me.' (Mt. 19:21)

Jesus isn't simply talking about what we get after death here; after all, what possible difference would giving everything we've got away have on our chances of getting to heaven? No, Jesus' response to the man is just as much about life: life here and now, life for others and a more meaningful and kingdom-focused life for us. Jesus' call to 'come' involves a positive challenge to live differently, plus the bonus of knowing him more closely. When it comes to action, Jesus says 'go' rather than 'stop'. Serving the poor means reviewing your choices in order to bring greater freedom to others and to yourself – it has less to do with restricting your lifestyle, denying yourself or holding back on action. We may not all be called to 'go and sell everything we own', but we are all called to 'do' for the sake of others, regardless of the cost to us.

What can I give?

So what about you, how would you describe your willingness to give? Matthew 19:16–30 represents one of two connected excerpts from Jesus' life, the other being verses 13–15 that precedes it. In three of the four gospels we meet three types of people. We've already met the rich man. He's a 'min in/max out' sort of person. He wants minimum effort for maximum effect. He thinks that as long as he follows the law he'll be sorted. In the world's eyes he's a success – he had it all! In God's eyes he was only prepared to give what he needed to, i.e. as little as possible to get by. Unfortunately, the chances are that the impact of his life, and indeed his own sense of fulfilment, will be minimal. The second type of people we meet are the disciples, who are shocked at the thought of a rich man's exclusion from

God's kingdom: '...they were greatly astonished and asked, "Who then can be saved?"' (Mt. 19:25).

The disciples can't believe the rich may not 'make it', people who historically had been associated as being 'under God's blessing'. If a rich man can't make it, how could they? Unlike the rich man, the disciples are 'max in/max out' people, as Peter is quick to point out in verse 27: 'We have left everything to follow you.' They've given 110 per cent and Jesus promises they'll receive back even more. In the world's eyes they may seem a little bit mad; they give away everything even though there's no guarantee of getting anything in return. In God's eyes the disciples have what they need, they give what they have, and they will get everything.

The third type of people we meet are children (Mt. 19:13-15), who are often 'max in/min out' in terms of effort. They seem to put the most effort in and yet initially get the least out. They don't always get the desired outcome, as much as they try. Whether it's learning to talk, walk or ride a bike, our children often find that their best efforts, frustratingly, are not enough. Yet when they first learn to mumble, stumble or fall off, they have the determination to get right back up and try again. In the world's eyes, children start life with very little to offer in terms of output, but in God's eyes they give what they can, and in most cases get what they need. It's the childlike qualities of trust, love, commitment, resilience, hope and an ambition to do better, that perhaps Jesus is highlighting as the things God is looking for in people who want to live in the way his kingdom requires – to be children of God who respond positively to him as their ruler and who see his people as his most treasured possession.

Childlike faith

Later in Matthew's account of Jesus' life, another man asks a similar question about life, and again it concerns the commandments:

Introduction

> 'Teacher, which is the greatest commandment in the Law?' Jesus replied: '"Love the Lord your God with all your heart and with all your soul and with all your mind." This is the first and greatest commandment. And the second is like it: "Love your neighbour as yourself."' (Mt. 22:36-39)

To enter into what Jesus would describe as 'life' (Mt. 19:17), we are simply commanded to love God, love others and, finally, love ourselves. The question of who exactly those 'others' are is something we'll start to address in Chapter 1, but for now let's concentrate on what we ought to do. The book *Mister God, This is Anna* provides a unique insight into what exactly a child's view of God, Christianity and life is all about. Anna lives as though God were her best friend, her soul mate and her ever-present help – which, of course, he is. Anna's understanding of God's desire for her life is particularly interesting: 'I know to love Mister God and to love people and cats and dogs and spiders and flowers and trees...' When Anna is asked by the local parson if she's a Christian, her reply is positive; when she is asked whether she reads the Bible or attends church, her response is a little less ordinary, as her friend and author of the book recalls:

> The message of the Bible was simple and any half-wit could grasp it in thirty minutes flat! Religion was for doing things, not for reading about things. Once you have got the message there wasn't much point in going over and over the same old ground... You went to church when you were very little. Once you got it, you went and did something about it. Keeping on going to church was because you hadn't got the message, or didn't understand it.[1]

Of course the support of a Christian community, whether that's a church, house group or family, is essential if we're to grow our faith, but maybe a child's understanding of what Christianity ought to look like in action is closer to Jesus' view than we think. The challenge for us is to find ways to capitalize on the energy, enthusiasm and simplicity of what it means to be a childlike Christian by providing ways by which we are able to express our faith in a real and effective way. Good habits established now, however simple, will stick with us for a lifetime. In response to the questions about what to do, Jesus' response to both the rich man and the teacher concerns the who. Love, the most frequently used word in Jesus' commands, is a verb, a doing word. We need to discover what we can do for the sake of God, ourselves and particularly for those others who are in need and with whom we share this whole wide world.

Your habits are someone's lifeline

As we've been writing this book it has inevitably caused us to consider our childhood and the kinds of people, shared experiences and activities that influenced our decisions then and have helped to form who we are now. The need to develop a sense of commitment and persistence to stick at it until things work out is the legacy of people like our piano teachers and cricket coaches. Naturally our parents, friends, schoolteachers, youth leaders and, more recently, each other have influenced many of the decisions we take daily. The person who seems to have had a lasting impact on Phil is his nan, and in particular an incident involving his feet and a towel when he was about five years old. He recalls how, as a child, his nan painstakingly taught him how to dry his feet in what may seem to us a rather structured and complicated way, but one which seems to work for him. Confused? Perhaps it would be better if he explained it:

> You may think that drying feet isn't that complicated but, like the origins of the universe, the existence of evil or blue cheese, to a confused five-year-old nothing is ever that simple. Nan would take the edge of the towel in one hand and systematically draw it in between each of my toes in turn as if she was threading a needle eight times over. As she did so, she would tell me that providing I always dried my feet in this way I would never have dry or flaky skin, cracked toes or sore feet. You can imagine

that the thought of my feet flaking away before my tweens was enough to convince me that it was a good idea to follow her advice. Twenty-five years on I still dry my feet in exactly the same way and, true to her word, I still own ten toes. More importantly than that, every time I begin to dry my feet after a shower or bath I remember my nan's words, her example to me, but most of all...I remember her.

It was probably the same with the disciples. Though the words Jesus spoke must have been powerful, it was most likely what he did that really made the difference to their lives. By his example he showed them what to do, and this would have been their lasting memory as they each embarked on their life from that point on. Some of the things he did were truly miraculous; others were far simpler and yet no less significant: 'Now that I, your Lord and Teacher, have washed your feet, you also should wash one another's feet. I have set you an example that you should do as I have done for you' (Jn. 13:14-15).

The point of this book is to provide you, and particularly your children, with shared experiences of simple lifestyle choices and activities, which in time we hope will become your habits of a lifetime. Every day for the next 25 years and beyond, it is our prayer that when you and your child/ren go to turn on the tap, open the fridge door, pay for your food, try on a sweater or sit down to work through homework, you'd remember some of the activities within this book, some of your shared experiences, but most of all you'll remember the poor; remember always to act with their lives in mind.

1 Water and Sanitation

What follows is a series of devotions designed to enable your family to connect with the issues of water, sanitation and God's heart for the poor. Work through in order or choose as many or as few as seems appropriate to your context. Most of us, and in particular children, learn best by doing, so whilst some are reflective, the majority of these activities are practical. It is important that all family members are involved, not just the children, as actions which develop thinking and change habits are generally ones which we learn together and from one another.

Your devotions on water and sanitation will help you to:

1 measure how much water you use in an average day

2 understand how poorer communities access water

3 understand the impact of using water that is unsafe

4 develop a value for water

5 think about what a luxury good sanitation is

6 explore Jesus' model of how we ought to respond to people in need

7 take action on behalf of people around the world who don't have access to safe water and sanitation.

Your way in

Everyday situations that your child/ren might face, or natural conversations that you might have as a family, will provide some of the best ways in to exploring the issue of water and sanitation and the poor. Look out for things your child/ren say and do as they begin to widen their perspective of their whole wide world and use these as a stimulus or way in to the subject in question.

Water and Sanitation

WHAT YOUR CHILD/REN MIGHT...	
DO	**SAY**
Play with water, e.g. with water pistols, in paddling pools, etc.	'Why should I care about someone else?'
Learn to swim	'What's water got to do with me?'
Bathe	'Why do I need to drink?'
Use the toilet	'Why do I need to use the plug?'
Drink or not finish a drink	'Does water cost a lot?'
Leave the tap running when they brush their teeth	'Where does water come from?'
Forget to wash their hands before meals	'Where does my wee go when I flush the toilet?'
Forget to wash their hands after going to the toilet	'Why does water taste so horrible?'
Forget to flush the toilet	'Why do I need to wash my hands?'
Flush the toilet unnecessarily	'Why does it matter how much water I use?'

Devotion 1

WATER, WATER, EVERYWHERE?

AIMS: To identify and understand the need for water. To measure how much water you use in an average day.

What you ought to know

Water – we take it for granted. We use it for both essential and non-essential tasks. If we consider a normal day, most of us would probably:

- take a bath or shower
- clean our teeth – twice
- use the toilet
- wash the dishes – three times, or put the dishwasher on
- use water to clean or cook food
- wash clothes
- make hot or cold drinks.

Whilst it is generally agreed that in order to satisfy our basic needs we need about 15–20 litres of water per person per day, on average the actual figure we use in the UK is more like 135 litres – equivalent to almost two baths![2] And as a family? Well, if you consider yourself to be an average household, then you probably use an incredible 2586 litres of water every week – that's like 3500 bottles of wine![3] So why do we use so much? Well, in addition to what we 'need', many of us also have the luxury of being able to use water for what we'd probably describe as our 'leisure activities', things such as swimming, playing or watering the garden.

Water and Sanitation

What your family could do

Introduction: Over the period of a day measure how much water you use.

You will need: a large piece of paper, *Printable 1: Buckets* (CD-ROM), real bucket/s

Discuss the different things you use water for and list them on one side of a large chart. Estimate how much water in buckets you think you will use during the day. As you go through your day, add pictures of buckets to your chart as you use water. The key below will give you a rough idea of how much water the different tasks you have to do in a day take.

Task	Number of buckets of water
Bath	8 buckets [4]
Shower	3 buckets every five minutes.[5]
Power shower	Up to 27 buckets every five minutes.[6]
Brushing your teeth – leaving the tap running continually	1 bucket [7]
Toilet	1 bucket [8]
Washing the dishes	½ bucket [9]
Using the dish washer	Up to 3 buckets [10]

Using the washing machine

Remember to include water for cooking, drinking and washing hands. Perhaps you could keep a bucket under your sink in the kitchen and each time you use a smaller amount of water, e.g., to wash the dishes, boil your vegetables or to rinse your salad, add it to the bucket. Once it is full, add a bucket picture to the chart and start again.

PRAYER POINT
At the end of the day, discuss how much water you have actually used. Was it more or less than you imagined? What did you use water for the most? What things could you go without if your water was limited? Thank God for the water you have and what that enables you to do.

Water and Sanitation

Devotion 2

ALL AROUND THE WORLD

Aim: To develop an understanding of how poorer communities access water.

What you ought to know

In many poorer countries in the world it's up to the women and children to collect the water for their family. If they're fortunate, women may be able to collect water from a communal tap or pump, but often they will have to travel great distances to collect small amounts of water from a lake, river or well. Collecting water takes a lot of time, meaning that women cannot do other important tasks and girls don't go to school. Joyce Mbwilo lives in Uhambingeto in Tanzania. She is thirty years old and has five children. Until recently, Joyce had to walk 14 miles every day to fetch water for her family. Her children often couldn't go to school because they hadn't had a chance to wash, drink or eat. Joyce has effectively walked three times around the world during her lifetime. She explains:

> Before the water supply project started here, I used to get up right in the middle of the night, at midnight, take my bucket and go to fetch water. I was back at 10 am the next day. The water was just 20 litres in a bucket. My family were very many, so 20 litres was not much, but this is the life I first lived, before this new project came.

After locating a spring on a mountain, a Tearfund supported project was able to help the villagers of Uhambingeto install a system of pipes that now provides safe water for drinking, cooking and washing for Joyce's community. There are millions of people like Joyce and her family, living in thousands of communities, who would all benefit from the opportunity to begin to get themselves out of poverty – having water is just the start.

What your family could do

Introduction: Use *Photograph 1* to introduce how poorer communities live. Discuss and pray about water, by considering:

- what we need to remember
- what is incredible
- what is a challenge
- what is encouraging.

You will need: *Photograph 1* (Poster Pack/CD-ROM)

Allow children to collect as much information as they can from the photograph itself. Ask your child/ren to describe what they can see. Share the appropriate parts of Joyce's story with your family to aid understanding as you discuss the contents of the photograph.

- Joyce Mbwilo lives in Uhambingeto in Tanzania, a country in east Africa. She is 30 years old and has five children.
- Until recently, Joyce had to walk 14 miles every day to fetch water for her family, leaving at midnight and returning home at 10 in the morning.
- Sometimes her children couldn't go to school because they hadn't had a chance to wash, drink or eat.
- With the help of Joyce's community, a Tearfund supported project has been able to lay a network of pipes to transfer water from a mountain spring to the village.
- Joyce and her community now have access to safe water for drinking, cooking and washing.

Use your discussion to form the basis of your prayers, for example:

Remember – that water is a very valuable resource that we take for granted.

Incredible – that some people in poorer countries have to walk several miles to get water. Thank God that organizations, such as Tearfund, are helping these people.

Challenge – ask God to help you change how you think about and use water. Ask God to help you identify ways in which you could support the work that Tearfund is doing in order to bring change.

Encouraging – thank God for the resources we have readily available, that we do have water. Thank God for communal taps that people can use and the positive effects this has on people's everyday lives.

> **PRAYER POINT**
> Please refer to the above as an example. God speaks to us all differently. He may have said specific things to you as a family. Use the outline above as a structure for focus and prayer. It's easy to remember, just think R.I.C.E!

Devotion 3

SHAKE, RATTLE AND BOIL

AIM: To help children to understand the impact of using water that is unsafe.

What you ought to know

Most of us don't have to think about where water comes from or where it goes, we just use it. It comes straight out of our taps – which are everywhere, in our homes, our places of work and even outside for use in the garden. But what would we do if water weren't so readily available? And what if the water you could get wasn't safe to use? Water quality is a big problem for many people from poor countries. Not only do they lack access to a water supply, but also any water they are able to find may not be safe.

One-fifth of the world's population has no access to safe drinking water.[12] In Ikuvala, a village in Tanzania, people have to dig in the sand in a desperate attempt to find water. Changes in the climate – something we'll consider in the next chapter – mean that a dry riverbed is all that remains of their original water supply. Many children gather daily to dig for water to drink. Although many of us will have done something similar on the beach as a child, for the poor finding water is no fun; it's serious, it's a matter of life or death.

In Central America, one-third of the population is without safe drinking water.[13] They rely on sources that industry can pollute with impunity as they are denied access to the government-subsidized supplies of the piped network. This affects health – 80 per cent of illnesses in developing countries are related to water and excreta.[14]

Water and Sanitation

Kambona Mtrigili digs for water for use in constructing roads; other villagers use the same dirty water to drink.

What your family could do

Introduction: Use *Photograph 2* to discuss the impact of using unsafe water on people's lives.

You will need: *Photograph 2* (Poster Pack/CD-ROM), dirty water, clear plastic water bottle

Eleven-year-old Ziada, has been sent by her class teacher to go and collect water for her school. The school will use this to drink, to cook with and, if there is any left, to water the plants.

At appropriate points during the discussion use the information above to help your child/ren's thinking. Use the discussion points below.

- Describe what you can see
- What do you think Ziada will use her water for?
- What might happen if people drink water that is unsafe?
- Why do you think Ziada has to use this water?
- Explain how you feel about this situation.

PRAYER POINT

People collecting water just outside the community of Uhambingeto in Tanzania are encouraged to 'clean' whatever water they can find in the following way:

1 Give it a good shake in order to kill some of the germs.
2 Allow it to settle.
3 Leave it in the sun for one hour to boil.

Take a clear plastic water bottle and fill it with rain water:

1 Sit in a circle and pass the bottle around to each member of your family. Each person needs to shake it and think of a word which best describes the water.
2 Next, place the water in the centre of your group, let it settle and reflect on what you've been learning about water.
3 Leave it out, ideally in the sun, for about an hour. Return to it and discuss: 'Would we drink it?' Pray for people who are struggling to access safe water on a daily basis.

Devotion 4

WATER IS PRECIOUS
AIM: To develop a value for water.

What you ought to know

Every day 14,000 people die from diseases directly related to drinking contaminated water.[15] Some diseases are caused by consuming water contaminated with bacteria or parasites, or by water-based hosts, others are caused by insects breeding beside contaminated water or by inadequate sanitation. Lack of access to water and sanitation primarily affects the poorest of the poor, especially women. Imagine having to wait all day to go to the toilet and then having to walk to a field in the dark, fearful of attack. This is the daily nightmare that many women in poor countries face because they don't have a toilet in their homes or even access to public facilities. If they did it would be much better! Cultural modesty dictates that it is OK for men to openly defecate during daytime hours but not for women – they have to wait until night time.

Children are affected too. Every 15 seconds a child dies from water-related diseases because they have no access to safe water and a lack of education on sanitation and hygiene.[16] That's only a few seconds longer than it took to read these last three sentences! Some people in poor communities don't understand the links between hygiene and disease; they often don't realize that something as simple as poor hygiene can also cause life-threatening disease. After walking as much as ten hours to fetch their water and then having to survive the rest of the day with less than 8 litres you could understand if people in poor communities neglected simple tasks such as washing their hands after going to the toilet; after all, many people in the UK don't bother. However, the main reason people in developing countries don't wash their hands is because they don't know they should, whereas we in the UK do know. Of course the difference between someone who is poor not washing and you is that the consequences can be fatal.

What your family could do

Introduction: use the times your child/ren naturally use the bathroom, e.g. washing their hands after they've been to the toilet or when they clean their teeth to think about how easy it is to forget how fortunate we are to have such facilities.

You will need: to clean your teeth, toothbrush, toothpaste, to wash your hands, water, basin, plug.

Illustration: Phil Bowyer

When you brush your teeth or wash your hands, put the plug in and find out how much water you use if you leave the water running for the duration. Compare this with how much water you use if you turn the tap off while brushing your teeth or washing your hands. Hopefully, changing how we behave towards water will impact our thinking about its true value.

PRAYER POINT
Tearfund partners have calculated that people living in poor communities around the world can survive on less than one bucket of water per person per day, about the same as you use if you brush your teeth and don't use a plug! Pray and think about people without sufficient water as you use your water throughout the coming week.

Water and Sanitation

Devotion 5

SPEND A PENNY

AIM: To understand the luxury of good sanitation.

What you ought to know

When people talk about sanitation for poor communities they're not talking about en suite facilities with flush toilets, but basic sewers, septic tanks, pour-flush latrines, or even just simple pit latrines.[17] Basic sanitation is about people knowing to wash their hands after use and being able to access a private toilet that safely disposes of excreta. It's the kind of thing most us take for granted. The kind of thing most of us do daily – even if we often don't like to talk about it! But talk about it we must. What's more shocking – the fact that nearly half the world's population has no access to sanitation, or the fact that over half of us use it?

The worst effects of the water and sanitation crisis are shocking because they are preventable. The terrible health record of developing countries could be rewritten with investment in water and sanitation. Many Tearfund partners are involved in water projects and, as the following example shows, education, sanitation and community involvement are crucial to their success.

Kigezi is a fertile and hilly corner of south-west Uganda where the problem is not so much scarcity as lack of access. Some people live high in the mountains, far from water sources, while elsewhere, people live in the valleys where the water source is in the hills. Streams and unprotected springs are often contaminated. Tearfund partner, The Kigezi Diocese Water and Sanitation Programme, has worked with local communities and women's groups to provide hundreds of hill-top homes with water jars, which collect rainwater from gutters. It is also piping water from hillside springs to taps in the valley, where people farm, as well as helping communities improve pit latrines and protect springs. Local people are involved in construction, trained in pump maintenance and educated in health and sanitation issues. Thousands of people now have better water – and they're using more of it.

Families in Kigezi, south-west Uganda are now able to access water thanks to the work of Tearfund's partner, The Kigezi Diocese Water and Sanitation Programme.

What your family could do

Introduction: think about ways in which you can help people who are trying to provide safe water and sanitation to communities who need it most.

You will need: empty water bottle, *Printable 2: 'Spend a penny'* label (CD-ROM)

Place a bottle or an empty jar by your toilet and every time you 'pay a visit' to the toilet, not forgetting to wash your hands first, pop in a penny or any other spare change you might have. Print off *Printable 2: 'Spend a penny'* label, encourage your child/ren to colour it in and stick it to your bottle (laminating it or covering it in clear sticky tape will help to keep it dry). Not only will it make you think about how much water you use and how much you take it for granted, but also it won't be long before you have enough to send off to Tearfund's Water and Public Health Fund to support projects like the ones Tearfund is operating in Kigezi. You'll be surprised at how quickly it all adds up.

Explain what you are going to do and why you are doing this as a family. Use the points below to help you structure your discussion:

- Nearly half the world has no access to sanitation.
- Sanitation is about people being able to access a private toilet that safely disposes of their waste and knowing to wash their hands after use.
- By putting a penny in the jar each time we use our bathrooms or toilets we can help people to get their own.

Once your bottle is full, empty the coins out, bank them and send a cheque to Tearfund along with your 'Spend a penny' label.

> **PRAYER POINT**
> Share the story of Tearfund partners working in Kigezi with your family. Pray for partners and projects that are committed to providing safe water and sanitation where it's needed most. Check out www.tearfund.org for more details.

Devotion 6

THE STORY OF THE GOOD SAMARITAN

AIM: To help children to explore Jesus' model of how we ought to respond to people's needs.

What you ought to know

A project supported by Tearfund in Tanzania has gone to great lengths in order to respond to the needs of the families who live in the district of Kilolo. Members of the Sustainable Development Project at Kilolo crossed over difficult terrain and walked for days and days through thick vegetation in order to locate a suitable natural spring at the foot of a hill. This is a point where rainfall that falls on the hill and filters down through the soil and rock eventually bubbles it's way to the surface. More arduous walking was required before the project was able to find the best route to lay the miles of pipe work that is needed to take this fresh water to the 10,000 people who together form four of the villages at Kilolo. The project is now helping villagers to install filters of gravel and sand and a network of pipes, which it estimates will provide each person with the 15 litres of water they need per day in order to survive. With local maintenance, this will provide clean water for many years to come.

It is important that we play our part in helping those we see in need just like the Samaritan did in Luke 10:25-37. The Samaritan did not walk past the man; he did not pretend he hadn't seen him. Instead he took the time to see what was wrong with the man and acted on what he saw. We must think and ask ourselves: What would Jesus do? We need to see things as Jesus sees them, with his compassion. We need to seek what God is asking us to do.

On our own we can't change the world, but working with others and through organizations, every one of us can make our voice heard and make a difference like the Samaritan did. Reflect on what you have learnt and what God has revealed to you. As a family you may want to record this in either picture or word form.

What your family could do

Introduction: Read together the Parable of the Good Samaritan in Luke 10:25-37, focusing particularly on verses 33-35:

> Then a Samaritan travelling down the road came to where the hurt man was lying. He saw the man and felt very sorry for him. The Samaritan went to him and poured olive oil and wine on his wounds and bandaged them. He put the hurt man on his own donkey and took him to an inn. At the inn, the Samaritan took care of him. The next day, the Samaritan brought out two silver coins and gave them to the innkeeper. The Samaritan said, 'Take care of this man. If you spend more money on him, I will pay it back to you when I come again.' [18]

You will need: a children's Bible: for younger children try Nick Butterworth and Mick Inkpen's *The Good Stranger*, published by Marshall, Morgan and Scott; for older children try the *International Children's Bible*, published by Authentic Media.

Key questions to discuss as a family:
- Why was the man in the story in need?
- Why couldn't he help himself?
- Explain why you think all those people passed by.
- What caused the Samaritan to stop? Why do you think he didn't walk on like the others?
- What sort of things did the Samaritan do? What did it cost him?
- Have you ever met anyone who needed help? What did you do?
- Do you know any other people who need your help?

PRAYER POINT

Draw pictures or make a list of some of the different people that you know who might need your help. Mount your drawings or list on coloured paper and place them somewhere prominent. Next time you pass, use them as a sign to:

- remind you about people who are in need
- stop and pray for them
- ask God to reveal the best ways of supporting and helping them.

Illustration: Matt Lomax

Devotion 7

SAVE WATER, SAVE LIVES?

AIMS: To recognize ways in which we could make better use of the water and sanitation we have. To inspire families to respond and take action on behalf of people around the world who don't have sanitation and safe water.

What you ought to know

A change in your attitude towards water, and any water saving habits you begin to develop as a result, is a great start as we seek to do what we can to make the world whole. However, the lives of millions of people the world over will not be changed unless you continue to think beyond yourselves. If as a result of this chapter all you do is make better use of the safe water and sanitation that your family has, then the impact you have on poor communities around the world who lack such luxuries will be limited. Once you've realized how much you take water for granted, our prayer is that you'll be motivated to take action for the sake of others who can't.

In recent years, the Government has responded well to campaigns to improve the world's ability to access water and sanitation. Prior to the World Summit on Sustainable Development held in August 2002, Water Matters, a joint campaign by Tearfund and WaterAid, urged the UK government to ensure that water and sanitation issues were a priority. At the time, Deputy Prime Minister John Prescott accepted more than 120,000 signatures to the Water Matters petition at No.10 Downing Street. The summit agreed new targets and programmes of action for the world's poorest people, notably a target to halve the proportion of people without access to sanitation by 2015. This was a vital step in a process that will ultimately change the lives of millions. It seems that the Water Matters campaign was a success.

Following further campaigning and lobbying by Tearfund and others, World Water Day on 22 March 2005, saw Hilary Benn announce a doubling of water and sanitation aid to Africa. Campaigning works, but there's still a lot to do. The challenge for the world community is to make sure that we continue to see practical action.

What your family could do

Introduction: Changes to our lifestyle habits are great, but alongside prayer and giving money we need to find other ways to encourage practical action which further impacts the lives of people from other countries.

You will need: Water charts from Devotion 1, writing/drawing materials.

Using your water charts, think about and discuss ways to make better use of the water that is available to you in your home. Here are just a few ideas to get you started:

In the kitchen
- Always try to use the plug and don't let the tap run when you're washing your hands or washing up.
- When you're washing up or peeling vegetables, use a bowl rather than the sink.
- Strain away any fats and food scraps from your dishwater and use the remaining water on your plants. It won't harm your plants. In fact, this type of water is excellent for getting rid of bugs.

In the bathroom
- Take a shower instead of a bath – this can save over 300 litres of water a week. Be careful though, a power shower can use more water than a bath![19]

- Turn off the tap when brushing your teeth – you could save 8 litres per minute.[20]
- Try placing a cut-down plastic bottle filled with water in your cistern. If the bottle holds half a litre of water, that's how much water you'll save with each flush (some local water authorities offer free Save-a-Flush devices to cut down on water – contact yours to see how to get one).

In the world

- If you have a water metre, saving water will save the person paying the bill money – money that reinvested wisely could save someone else's life. Agree as a family that you will send the money you save on your water bill to Tearfund to support water work in poor communities.

> **HELPFUL HINT**
> The energy it takes to purify water before and after we use it also has consequences for our climate – something we'll get on to in the next chapter. Saving water could be your first step to reducing climate change and saving the planet.

- As a family, use your water saving actions as a way to begin to think about how you could start to save the lives of others. Discuss and write a simple letter, or draw a picture, which you could send to your Member of Parliament. Ask them to make sure that the UK Government continues to increase aid to water and sanitation and persuades other rich governments to do the same. Make it personal; tell them about some of the lifestyle changes that you have committed to.

PRAYER POINT

Every time you flush, think about other areas in your home, at work, or at school, where you could save water and pray for others who don't have that choice. Pray for governments who could make a difference to people who lack access to safe water and sanitation, think about ways that you could continue to make life different for them too.

2 Weather and Energy

What follows is a series of devotions designed to enable your family to connect with the issues of weather, climate change and God's heart for the poor. Work through in order or choose as many or as few as seems appropriate to your context. Most of us, and in particular children, learn best by doing, so whilst some are reflective, the majority of these activities are practical. It is important that all family members are involved, not just the children, as actions that develop thinking and change habits are generally ones that we learn together and from one another.

Your devotions on weather and energy will help you to:

1. understand how the weather impacts people from poorer communities
2. identify and understand how we use energy and what affect it might be having on our world
3. develop an understanding of the effect transport has on the weather
4. think about the ways in which reducing, reusing and recycling what we consume could make a difference
5. think about how our lifestyle choices impact the poor
6. understand how climate change impacts people's lives
7. consider alternative ways of having fun without using energy.

Your way in

Everyday situations that your child/ren might face, or natural conversations that you might have as a family, will provide some of the best ways in to exploring the issue of weather, energy, climate change and the poor. Look out for things your child/ren say and do as they begin to widen their perspective of their whole wide world and use these as a stimulus or way in to the subject in question.

WHAT YOUR CHILD/REN MIGHT...

DO	SAY
Leave lights on when they're not in the room	'Why do disasters happen?'
Leave the TV on	'Why is it so hot/wet/cold today?'
Use the standby button on the remote	'Do we have to walk to school?'
Leave the fridge door open	'Why can't we use the car?'
Play with electronic games	'Why don't those people on TV have any homes?'
Prefer to be driven than to walk/cycle	'Where do the refuse collectors put our rubbish?'
Leave toys on and forget to turn them off	'Can people really make things out of our old rubbish?'
Throw food in the bin	
Waste paper	'Do plants really like to eat other plants?'
Like to take a trip to the bottle bank	'How do people get small enough to get in my TV?'
	Various questions about how you use energy

HELPFUL HINT

Tearfund's booklet *For tomorrow too* is a pocket-sized lifestyle guide with lots of suggestions on how you can cut your personal contribution to climate change. To order your free copy call 0845 355 8355 (ROI +44 845 355 8355).

Weather and Energy

Devotion 1
SWEPT AWAY

AIM: To understand how the weather impacts people from poorer communities.

What you ought to know

For many of us, the first time we begin to consider whether we ought to respond to the needs of the poor is when we're made aware of some kind of disaster, whether that be earthquakes, famines or floods. You may not have noticed, but over the last 50 years the number of natural disasters occurring worldwide has more than doubled.[21] Scientists predict that owing to changes in our climate, many of the areas that currently endure severe climatic conditions, like droughts and floods, will be subject to an increased ferocity and frequency of such weather events. Least able to adapt and prepare for further changes to the climate, the poor suffer more than any of us. Lack of choice means they often live in dangerous places vulnerable to disasters. A slum community on a riverbank is more vulnerable to flooding than a prosperous Western town, with well-built brick houses, flood defences and sophisticated early warning systems. Even though disasters caused by changes in our climate do touch our lives, we generally have the ability to recover.

Nur Mohammed's family home has been swept away a number of times in recent years. Storms and fierce currents are biting huge chunks out of the island where he lives – Hatiya Island, off the south coast of Bangladesh – and it's getting worse. Nur Mohammed says: 'The island is breaking up faster than before. There are big storms more often. The place where we used to live is now at least a kilometre out to sea.'[22]

Bangladesh is particularly vulnerable because it's a delta for some of Asia's biggest rivers. Erosion is getting worse as more

Nur Mohammed and his family have twice lost their home, swept away by storms and strong currents.

and more water and floods pour down the rivers into the sea. Most of Bangladesh is less than a couple of metres above sea level. Global average sea level has already risen by 0.2 metres. If this continues, millions of people in Bangladesh and other low-lying areas will lose their homes and land.

What your family could do

Introduction: Get your children to build their own shelter. Children love building den's in their rooms so they'll enjoy this.

You will need: old cardboard, plastic sheeting, mats, wooden poles or canes, *Photograph 3* (Poster Pack/CD-ROM)

Build a shelter. If the weather is good, why not build it outside. This is exactly the sort of housing that very poor people live in – some because they are very poor, and others because they have lost their normal house in a disaster. Encourage your children to spend some time in the shelter trying to imagine what it must be like living there, without knowing how long it will last or when the next disaster will hit. Encourage them to stick their questions, thoughts and prayers to the 'walls' of the inside.

Use *Photograph 3* to relate Nur Mohammed's situation to your children. Use the following points to summarize his story:

The Whole Wide World

Weather and Energy

- Nur Mohammed and his family live in Bangladesh in a dangerous place.
- In fact his home has been swept away a number of times in recent years.
- Storms and water are breaking up the island where he lives
- The place where he used to live is now at least a kilometre ($2/3$ of a mile) out to sea.

Try to imagine how your family would feel if your home was swept away.

> **PRAYER POINT**
> Use your discussion to lead into prayer. Pray for Nur Mohammed's community and people living in countries such as Bangladesh as they prepare to face bad floods that may come at any time. Thank God that he offers refuge to everyone, whether they're poor or rich, and that he promises to save us if we believe in Jesus. Pray for those you know who are going through difficult times, that God will be close to them and bring them refuge.

Devotion 2

ENERGY AT HOME

AIMS: To identify and understand how we use energy. To begin to consider how the way we live affects the world.

What you ought to know

Energy, in the form of electricity or gas is readily available to us and, like water, we often take it for granted. Many of us are guilty of consuming too much energy too often. All this supply on demand comes at a great cost to poor communities around the world, who are often the first to pay the price for our endless production and consumption. Scientific evidence shows that the increasing levels of non-renewable energy we're using are causing a rise in the world's temperature and the kinds of changes to the climate that families like Nur Mohammed's are experiencing.

Greenhouse gases, such as carbon dioxide (CO_2), nitrous oxide and methane, which are naturally present in our atmosphere, create a barrier that traps the sun's energy and keeps the earth warm. However, when we use energy, for example to heat our homes or produce electricity, the fossil fuels we burn (coal, oil and natural gas) lead to an 'enhanced greenhouse effect' by thickening the barrier and causing temperatures to rise unnaturally. This in turn leads to climate change.[23] Rising temperatures are not the only result; the climate is affected in lots of different ways – for example the number and severity of extreme weather events like floods, droughts and heatwaves increase, and sea-levels rise.

Many of the lifestyle choices we make daily affect the climate and put pressure on the global ecosystem. Just think about some of the inventions we've seen over the last century, most of which need some form of energy to enable them to work. We use energy to heat our homes, to power our lights, to link us to the World Wide Web. Around 25 per cent of all CO_2 emissions released into the atmosphere from the UK come from the energy used to run our homes.[24] Even if we have not yet worked out how to control the weather, rain or shine, it seems we may be able to affect it.

What your family could do

Introduction: The average UK home produces six tonnes of CO_2 every year; any reduction here could significantly slow down climate change.[25] Spend some time thinking about how energy gets used by your family.

You will need: sticky notes

Set your family the task of going through the house and putting a sticky note on everything that needs electricity to make it work. Remember to include items that need batteries. At the end collect all the sticky notes and count up the number of items that use electricity. Explain that every time we use electricity we add carbon dioxide to the atmosphere, which makes the world's temperature rise.

The cleanest and most sustainable way to reduce our personal contribution to climate change is simply to use less energy. As a family, try to identify ways in which you could use less energy and make changes. Below are a few possibilities:

- Watch TV together as a family rather than everyone watching in separate rooms.
- Switch off appliances. Even when they are on standby some models of TVs, PCs and stereos use between 40 and 70 per cent of the energy they use when switched on.[26]
- Cook meals together and eat as a family more often to save on the energy you use whilst cooking.
- Open the curtains, let in more natural light and cut down on unnecessary use of lights.[27]

- Shut your fridge door quickly – for every minute it's open it takes three minutes of energy to cool it down again.[28]

At least two tonnes of the CO_2 that your home releases will probably come from 'dirty' electricity generators, i.e. those which burn fossil fuels and so produce lots of greenhouse gases.[29] However, not all energy is bad. By switching to a 'green' electricity provider, i.e. those that use renewable energy sources like sun and wind that don't produce any harmful gases, you can actually help slow the process of climate change and still use energy.[30]

PRAYER POINT
Identify which changes to the way you use energy you could make today in order to positively impact tomorrow's climate. Pray a prayer of commitment to begin to explore and make positive changes to the way your family uses energy from now on. Involve your children – why not make your own fridge magnets, which could not only act as responsive prayers but also serve as daily reminders to save energy.

HELPFUL HINT
Good Energy claims to be the only UK company obtaining all its electricity from renewable sources, including wind, sun and water. By switching to Good Energy you can also raise money for Tearfund. For every household that switches, Tearfund receives £20, and another £10 one year on. Call 0845 456 1640 or visit www.good-energy.co.uk to find out more. Just quote GE38.

Weather and Energy

Devotion 3

PLANES, TRAINS AND AUTOMOBILES

AIMS: To develop an understanding of the effect of transport on the world. To identify ways in which we can make a difference.

What you ought to know

The fuel we use to power cars, trains and planes are fossil fuels and so they produce greenhouse gases when we use them. Transport in the UK is the fastest growing source of CO_2, accounting for about one-quarter of our total emissions.[31] The growth in budget European airlines and the increasingly popularity of short overseas breaks means greenhouse gas pollution due to air travel is increasing. Reducing short-haul trips, which are more environmentally polluting per passenger kilometre than longer trips, is one way we can positively affect climate change. If you do have to fly it is possible to offset your emissions by donating to organizations that will plant trees, invest in renewable energy and research into energy efficiency on your behalf.[32]

Illustration: Andy Baldwin

Taking the train for shorter trips, instead of flying or driving, will cut down on pollution. In fact, for shorter trips public transport in general is less damaging to the environment than cars. If you can't use public transport, car sharing is a good

50 The Whole Wide World

alternative. Joining friends to and from school or on a night out will make a real difference. Of course walking is even better: it not only reduces pollution but could also save you money. Trips to the local shop, going to church, getting to football practice or travelling to school could all provide great walking opportunities. Cycling is also good news for slowing climate change – and it keeps you fit.[33]

What your family could do

Introduction: Explore different forms of transport and begin to think about how the ones you use increase your energy consumption and therefore the rate of climate change.

You will need: *Printable 3: Modes of transport* (CD-ROM)

Split the images showing different forms of transport into two sets.

SET ONE – motorbikes, cars, lorries, buses, etc.

SET TWO – bike, walking, running, etc.

Discuss each set in turn, thinking about what they have in common. Move on to consider how the two sets are different. Encourage your child/ren to colour them in. Explain that every time we use fuel we add carbon dioxide to the atmosphere, which makes the world's temperature rise.

> **PRAYER POINT**
> Thank God that we can make a big difference to the poor by making small changes to our lifestyle. Think about how, as a family, you could reduce the amount of fuel you use – when could you walk or cycle? Why not make a family key rack, or prayer fobs for your keys, which display prayers or questions such as 'Do I really need to take the car today?'

Weather and Energy

Devotion 4

WASTE

AIM: To understand the connection between our waste and the weather. To think about the impact of reducing, reusing and recycling what we consume.

What you ought to know

It's not just what we use that is impacting our climate but what we don't use. Around 80 per cent of the rubbish we throw away in the UK goes straight into landfill sites, which, as well as emitting CO_2, are also the second largest source of methane emissions.[34] The UK currently recycles just 8 per cent of its household waste, even though 70 per cent of the waste in our dustbins could be recycled![35]

Here are three steps to take towards cutting down on the energy we waste through our rubbish:

1. Reduce

It's important to think about ways to reduce the amount of waste we produce in the first place. Things like stopping unwanted junk mail being sent to you or reducing the number of plastic bags you use by choosing a fabric or reusable bag will help.[36]

2. Reuse

We should also think about how we can reuse household goods, rather than just throwing them in the bin, for example reuse envelopes by sticking labels over the address. Buy rechargeable items, such as batteries and cameras, instead of disposable ones. Buy products such as washing powder in refillable containers. Take your old clothes and books to charity shops.

3. Recycle

Composting your organic waste, which is the main source of methane in landfills, is the most efficient way to reduce emissions. Turn your food scraps and tea bags into compost and return the nutrients and energy back to the soil where they can be reused.[37] Make the most of local recycling facilities for plastic, glass, paper and tin cans.

What your family could do

Introduction: Save your rubbish for a week. See what kind of things you waste and what changes you could make to impact the climate.

You will need: a variety of rubbish

Sort your rubbish into two groups depending on what can and what cannot be recycled. Items that can be recycled are:

- aluminium cans
- paper and card
- glass bottles and jars
- tins and cans
- clear plastic bottles and containers
- foil.

HELPFUL HINT

Food and vegetable waste is something that will be covered in Chapter 3, Devotion 7. It is not recommended to include this kind of waste is this particular activity.

Visually this should show how much of what we throw away could be recycled and the difference we can make.
- Discuss what happens to the rubbish.
- Discuss why we should recycle.
- Discuss how we can reduce the amount of packaging we use.

PRAYER POINT

Encourage your children to make 'reduce', 'reuse' and 'recycle' labels for collection boxes. Label up the boxes accordingly and start reducing, reusing and recycling your waste. They could make a start by writing simple prayers on each box. They could be prayers of commitment or a thought about ways to improve ways to save rubbish.

Devotion 5

THE STORY OF THE WISE AND FOOLISH BUILDERS

AIM: To think about how our lifestyle choices impact the poor.

What you ought to know

The parable of the Wise and Foolish Builders (Mt. 7:24-27) is a great visual story of the consequences of following Jesus, but also can be used to illustrate some of the effects of climate change.

You could be forgiven for thinking the person who builds their home on the sand is similar to someone who is poor and chooses to live in a vulnerable community, perhaps on a riverbank, steep slope or in an earthquake zone – but you'd be wrong. In actual fact, many of our lifestyle choices mean that we are camped firmly in the foolish category, because we're often wasteful people whose actions bring disasters to the doorsteps of the poor and the vulnerable.

Those who build on good foundations are those that obey the Lord Jesus, i.e. they are more concerned about seeing justice done than gathering things for themselves, they serve God rather than money, they make generous decisions which positively impact others and not just themselves. If we live our lives like that – not being greedy and selfish and demanding so much energy – we will be freed to bless the poor who suffer because of our selfishness. Using greener energy, i.e. energy that uses renewable sources like sun and wind, or using less energy, is a vital part of what it means to be a disciple of Jesus these days.

We have to be wise. We need to live wisely and make lifestyle changes that will benefit others. Thank God that we can afford to be wise and change the world we live in. Consider simple and yet effective lifestyle changes you may need to make in order to impact the climate.

What your family could do

Introduction: Read together the Parable of the Wise and Foolish Builders (Mt. 7:24–27). Split it into two parts.

You will need: a children's Bible: for younger children try Nick Butterworth and Mick Inkpen's *The House on the Rock*, published by Marshall, Morgan and Scott; for older children try the *International Children's Bible*, published by Authentic Media, Photograph 4 (Poster Pack/CD-ROM).

Part 1 – The wise man (verses 24 and 25)
Everyone who hears these things I say and obeys them is like a wise man. The wise man built his house on the rock. It rained hard and the water rose. The winds blew and hit that house. But the house did not fall, because the house was built on the rock.[38]

Read and then consider what made the man in the story wise.

Part 2 The foolish man (verses 26 and 27)
But the person who hears the things I teach and does not obey them is like a foolish man. The foolish man built his house on the sand. It rained hard, the water rose, and the winds blew and hit that house. And the house fell with a big crash.[39]

Read and then consider what made the other man in the story foolish.

Key questions to discuss as a family:
- Why did the house on the rock stand; why did the man build it there?
- Why did the house on the sand crash; why did the man build it there?

- Where would you build your house? What if you had no choice?
- What do you think are the reasons people build their houses in dangerous places today? Think back to Devotion 1 and Nur Mohammed's story.
- Discuss stories of people in the news, or that you know, whose houses have been destroyed in the same way as the story Jesus told? What did you do?

PRAYER POINT

Look at *Photograph 4*. Discuss how people in poor countries live. What would it be like? Pray for people who are faced with the threat of disasters due to climate change. Ask God to help you to respond to people's needs and to commit to lifestyle changes that could make a difference to the poor.

Weather and Energy

Devotion 6

JUST DESERT

AIM: To see how climate change impacts people.

What you ought to know

In the dried-up region of the Sahel in Niger, West Africa, the human face of climate change is plain to see. The Tuareg nomads are used to making a living amidst the dust and droughts, but recently even they have found it tough. The rains have been less reliable and the droughts more severe. They are used to moving on to find new pasture, but as rainfall declines, more herders are forced to compete for the same grass. As a result, some Tuareg families have gradually lost their animals and headed for the cities in search of income, but this is a last resort.

Jemed, a Tearfund partner for the last fifteen years, is working to transform the lives of many Tuareg families. To enable communities to adapt to their changing environment, Jemed helps to create 'fixation points'. Based around a permanent well, 'fixation points' provide families with an opportunity to loan animals and to develop various services, which together will help to improve family life. Literacy training, health training, sewing circles and primary schools all help and provide the community with the skills they need to better meet the future challenges. Although Tuareg women spend most of the year at the fixation point, families are still able to retain their nomadic culture – the men still travel with their animals to find pasture as they have done for centuries.

Fixation points help Tuareg families to face up to the impact of changes in their climate today as well as prepare them for what may happen in the future.

Jemed also helps people harness the rain by building long low walls across wide dry riverbeds. When the rains eventually come the water is slowed down and soaks into the parched land. Trees and bushes grow either side of the dykes for up to a kilometre, providing pasture for their livestock over the dry season. Jemed is not afraid to explain its Christian beliefs to the Tuareg; many see Jemed's practical help as a demonstration of the God of the Bible – some families have become Christians.

What your family could do

Introduction: Use *Photograph 5* to explore how climate change affects the lives of people all over the world.

You will need: *Photograph 5* (Poster Pack/CD-ROM)

Allow children to collect as much information as they can from the three photographs. Ask your child/ren to describe what they can see. Use your discussion to form the basis of your prayers, by considering:

- what we need to remember
- what is incredible
- what is a challenge
- what is encouraging.

For example:

Remember – that we can recycle many things, such as cans, paper, bottles, clothes and shoes.

Incredible – that how we are living is having such an impact on our world; people who are living in developing countries are suffering because of how we live. Thank God that we can afford to be wise and change the world we live in.

Challenge – ask God to help you change how you think about and use energy (electricity, gas and fuel) and to help you identify ways in which you could support the work that Tearfund is doing in order to bring change.

Encouraging – thank God for the resources that we have available, that we do have electricity that makes computers, microwaves, kettles, etc. work. Thank God for fuel that enables us to travel from one part of the world to another.

PRAYER POINT
Please refer to the above as an example. God speaks to us all differently. He may have said specific things to you as a family. Use the above as a structure for focus and prayer. It's easy to remember, just think R.I.C.E!

Devotion 7

DO SOMETHING LESS BORING INSTEAD

AIMS: To understand the value of energy. To show that there are alternative forms of entertainment.

What you ought to know

Climate change is not just a remote scientific theory. The world is getting hotter; it's showing signs of sickness. Global average surface temperatures have increased by 0.6°C during the twentieth century. If that continues it could rise by up to 5.8°C by 2100.[40] When we are ill with a fever, our body temperature changes from being normal to fever pitch. This tiny increase of 0.3°C switches us from feeling well to feeling sick. This sensitivity of the human body to temperature change is one way of appreciating the phenomenon of climate change.

To survive we all need to begin to respect our global environment more. It is predicted that if we continue to live the way we do, global temperatures and sea levels will continue to increase. As we have already considered, this causes extreme weather conditions in the form of floods, droughts and heat waves. The poor are suffering more than any of us. Lack of choice means they often live in dangerous places vulnerable to disasters.

We have all seen images on television and in newspapers of the effects of global warming, even if we have not directly experienced them. Disasters often bring about periods of national shock, reflection and openness to do things differently. Many of the disasters we see aren't that natural at all, but are caused by changes in the climate as a consequence of our activity. We need to think about the energy we use and change how we live. We need to reduce the energy we use in order to slow down climate change. We have a personal responsibility to become part of the solution.

What your family could do

Introduction: Try spending some time together as a family enjoying activities that don't require any energy.

You will need: games

Have a games afternoon. Turn off the TV, PlayStation, computer, CD player and enjoy spending time together. Spend an afternoon playing games that don't require any electricity, either inside or outside.

PRAYER POINT
You will need: inflatable globe

Roll or throw the globe to each other. The person holding the globe says a prayer and then passes it to another person.

- Start with thank-you prayers – these may be a word or phrase.
- Move on to asking prayers – ask God to help you with the specific lifestyle changes you have decided upon as a family.
- Finally, think and pray about the country the globe lands on.

If it is a poor country, pray for the conditions in which the people live. If it is a rich country pray for people to change how they are living in order for climate change to slow down. For this part of the activity you may want to work as a family.

3 Food

What follows is a series of devotions designed to enable your family to connect with the issues of food shortage and God's heart for the poor. Work through in order or choose as many or as few as seems appropriate to your context. Most of us, and children in particular, learn best by doing, so whilst some are reflective, the majority of these activities are practical. It is important that all family members are involved, not just the children, as actions that develop thinking and change habits are generally ones that we learn together and from one another.

Your devotions on food will help you to:

1 identify when, what and how much you eat
2 understand what happens when there is a lack of food
3 consider what it must be like to have no food
4 understand how difficult it is to get food
5 explore how Jesus provides for people's basic needs
6 consider how to use food responsibly
7 explore ways in which we can contribute to food provision.

Your way in

Everyday situations that your child/ren might face, or natural conversations that you might have as a family, will provide some of the best ways in to exploring the issue of food and the poor. Look out for things your child/ren say and do as they begin to widen their perspective of their whole wide world and use these as a stimulus or way in to the subject in question.

WHAT YOUR CHILD/REN MIGHT...

DO	SAY
Waste their food	'I'm starving!'
Leave their food	'But I'm not hungry anymore.'
Ask for something to eat and then change their minds	'I don't want it.'
Not eat	'Why don't you send my food to them if they don't have any?'
Eat too much	
Prefer sweets	'Do I have to eat it all?'
Fussy about what they eat	'But I don't like food shopping.'
Overeat when they're bored	'Why do we need food?'
Unbalanced diet	'How does food grow?'
Criticize or question what you eat	'But I don't like that.'
	'Do I have to eat my vegetables?'

Devotion 1

FOOD DIARY

AIMS: To identify when, what and how much you eat. To begin to understand that some people don't have the choices we have.

What you ought to know

If someone says the word 'food' what do you think of – your favourite or least favourite food? We have such a variety of foods to choose from. Go into any supermarket and you can buy food that will enable you to eat a balanced diet: fish, eggs, meat that provide sources of protein; bread, pasta, rice that are carbohydrates and give us the energy we need to get through the day; fruits and vegetables that are rich in vitamins and minerals and help to protect the body from illness; cakes, biscuits, sweets that contain sugars and fats that can make us unhealthy and overweight if we eat too much of them.

Food is essential for survival; without it we would die. Our bodies need fuel, fuel in the sense of food to enable them to work properly. Our children need to learn to eat a balanced diet in order to be healthy. To be healthy, we need to consume and absorb appropriate amounts of energy and all the nutrients our bodies require. Too little or too much of some, over a period of months or longer, may lead to ill health. In the UK some people choose to eat unhealthy diets, but in poorer countries people don't always have much choice and have to eat unhealthy diets.

One of Tearfund's evangelical Christian partners in Guatemala, the Life Association, works with local communities to set up health training programmes. Seventy-eight locally recruited health promoters work in the villages to help parents understand the effects of poor nutrition and the range of diet their families need. They also make sure children receive treatment for common infections. Felipe Par, aged twelve, is now well aware of the benefits of a healthy diet: 'I like eating spinach best of all, because it tastes good and makes me strong. When I grow up I'll be a strong man.'

A stronger, healthier generation of young children means the whole community benefits. How do you think your child/ren would respond to a bowl full of spinach?

What your family could do

Introduction: Think about the way you eat. Use this as an opportunity to explain that lots of people in other parts of the world don't have the choice to eat a balanced diet. Explore how this affects your attitudes towards food.

You will need: paper, writing/drawing materials

Keep a food diary for a week. As a family, either in words, pictures or both, keep a record of when you eat and what you eat. At the end of the week look back at your diary and discuss the foods you eat and how you eat regularly. Discuss:

- Why we need food – that it makes our bodies work.
- What might happen to us if we don't eat the right balance of foods.

Illustration: Andy Baldwin

In order to eat healthily it's recommended that we each eat five portions of fruit and vegetables per day (one portion is equal to roughly 80 grams). Make a commitment, as a family, to try to eat five portions of fruit or vegetables – try it for five days and see how it feels. As you do so, think about others who don't have the choices you have.

> **PRAYER POINT**
> Draw around your hand and for each of the five fingers write one prayer about food. Remember to include a prayer that gives thanks for the fact that you have food and one for those that don't.

Devotion 2

WHEN HUNGER STRIKES

AIM: To develop an understanding of how you feel and act when there is a lack of food.

What you ought to know

Just thinking about the range of foods you put in your shopping trolley probably makes you feel hungry. Unfortunately not everyone has the luxury of choosing what to eat. Just take a look at these frightening statistics:

- Nearly 800 million people in poor countries don't have enough to eat – that's roughly ten times the population of a country like Germany, the Philippines or Japan.[41]
- Over 200 million children aged under five in poor countries are malnourished.[42]
- 16,000 children die every day from chronic hunger and related diseases.[43]

It's ironic that as people in rich countries die of diseases caused by eating too much food, people in poor countries don't have enough to live on. Where poverty is a way of life, diet is often very restricted. If children don't get the food and nutrients they need, their malnutrition, literally their lack of nutrition, will begin to damage their health in some the following ways:

- **Wasting**: reduced weight for the child's age, usually due to acute (short-term) malnutrition
- **Stunting**: reduced height for age, due to chronic (long-term) malnutrition
- **Underweight**: reduced weight for age, usually due to both acute and chronic malnutrition.

As well as physical development, malnutrition reduces energy and prevents people from working; it impairs intellectual development; it can damage the body's immune system, cause night blindness, rickets or chest infections and can increase birth complications and maternal mortality. Dr. Axel Suquen, Executive Director of Tearfund's partner the Life Association says food shortages 'means people can't have dreams, can't build for the future, can't create. The poor end up being even poorer.'

What your family could do

Introduction: People need food to give them energy, but also to allow their bodies and brains to grow, as they should. People are more likely to suffer from diseases without the proper food.

You will need: to organize a family activity.

As a family do an activity that uses lots of energy, such as swimming. Afterwards discuss how you feel. Hopefully all your family will feel very hungry. Discuss what it would be like if there was little or no food available. How would this affect the rest of your day?

Take this opportunity to explain that for some people this is a fact of life, day after day, week after week – they don't have enough food to eat. This has a dramatic effect on their bodies: they lack energy, they don't grow as they should and, as a result, disease is more likely.

PRAYER POINT
Thank God together that you have food to eat. Think and discuss the kind of family prayer you think would be most appropriate to say together each time you eat.

The Par family from Guatemala give thanks for their lunch.

Devotion 3

GROW YOUR OWN

AIMS: To develop an understanding of what is needed to grow your own food. To begin to understand how difficult this sometimes is, even with the correct resources.

What you ought to know

Many people in poor countries are not able to feed themselves because they either lack access to land or any land they did have they have had to sell to find money in order to live. People sometimes lose what land they have through conflict or disasters, or owing to the kind of environmental problems that were discussed in the Chapter 2. It's hard to grow food in soil that has been damaged through deforestation, flooding and droughts. In poor countries, 60 per cent of families work the land and are dependent on water.[44] Around 94 per cent of crops are reliant on rainfall.[45] If there is too little rain, the effects can be devastating.

Some poor families may not have the skills or strength to work for an income with which to buy food. Pedro Par and his wife Antolin are fortunate: they are able to grow maize because the owner of their land accepts half of what they grow as rent. Many other families, even if they have land, are often unable to afford the tools, labour or seed to get an adequate crop. The knowledge and resources to increase yields may be beyond their reach. Tearfund's partner the Diocese of Ruaha, in Tanzania, operates a revolving loan scheme where families are able to apply for grants that enable them to invest in seeds and tools to grow crops. After their harvest they pay back their loan, reinvest any profits they may have made in next year's crop and, if they need to, reapply for another loan for the following year.

It gives families a real way to become self-sufficient. In Guatemala Tearfund's partner, Life Association, helps the Pars and other poor families to grow vegetables by providing them with seeds and training.

I didn't really know anything about growing vegetables from seeds,' says Pedro, 'but I went to a meeting in the village and heard about the seed distribution project and how we could participate in the programme.'

What your family could do

Introduction: Think about what it takes to grow your own food.

You will need: Photograph 6 (Poster Pack/CD-ROM), seeds, garden tools and lots of energy!

If you have a garden, develop part of it into a vegetable patch. As a family, take a trip to the garden centre to buy the seeds and tools you may need. Plant the seeds, water them and watch them grow!

Through this activity, you should be able to bring out the point that you needed a variety of things for the vegetables to grow. You needed seeds, tools, soil that is good enough for vegetables to grow in and water – this all needed a certain amount of energy and money. Using *Photograph 6*, share the story of Pedro's family.

- Some poor families may not have the skills or strength to work for an income with which to buy food.
- Pedro Par and his wife Antolin grow maize because the owner of their land accepts half of what they grow as rent.
- Tearfund's partner, Life Association, in Guatemala, helps the Pars and other poor families to grow vegetables by providing them with seeds and training.
- Now on the small piece of land where Pedro's family live they are able to grow vegetables.

Food

- Thanks to Tearfund, many families like Pedro's are able to add health-giving vegetables to their diet. Antolin sees the difference it makes: 'Since we've had our vegetable plot I've noticed a real change in our children – they don't get sick so often now.'

If you don't have outdoor space or window boxes, you could still grow something like cress. Although this is on a smaller scale you will need a certain amount of materials: cotton wool, yoghurt pot, seeds and plenty of water.

> **PRAYER POINT**
> As your crops grow, don't forget to pray for people in poor countries: families like Pedro's, who often don't have the land, the skills or strength to work the land to grow food. If they do have land, they might not be able to buy tools or enough seeds. They are unable to be self-sufficient. Pray for Tearfund partners like Life Association who are lending a hand and making a difference.

Devotion 4

LEND A COW

AIM: To explore how people in poverty are being given resources that can make their life easier. To explore ways we can contribute to food provision.

What you ought to know

Tangaye is a rural area of Burkina Faso where a lack of means of cultivation, drought and depleted soils has brought about a shortfall in food production. This has led to a steady urban drift and the break up of communities. Tearfund's partner the Evangelical Association Supporting Development (AEAD) has responded by establishing a successful ox-ploughing project to improve living standards and food security:

- increasing food production (yields and areas cultivated) and diversifying crops
- improving soil fertility through animal manure
- reducing the work burden for families, especially for women who can use the animals for transport
- providing cash income through the sale of trained oxen
- improving the skills of farmers through training in animal husbandry and ploughing
- vaccinating cattle against parasites.

A central part of the programme is an oxen loan scheme. Pairs of young bull oxen are purchased for participating families and trained to plough. Each family uses their two oxen for ploughing before selling them after three years. From the proceeds, three young oxen can be bought for training, one of which is given away to a new family joining the scheme. The number of cattle owned in the area has doubled in the last five years.

What your family could do

Introduction: Share Sidnomwende's story of how people use oxen to grow food in Burkina Faso by asking your child/ren to put the pictures in the correct order.

You will need: *Printable 4: Oxen pictures* (CD-ROM)

Cut out the pictures and let your child put them in the correct order.

Photos: Jim Loring/Tearfund

1 Plough the field with Oxen

2 Harvest the crops once they have grown

3 Store the crops in barns and put the rest in trees to feed the animals

4 Pound the millet to break it up

5 Grind it into a fine powder to get it ready for cooking

6 Cook the meal outside

7 Dinner time

The pictures explain how Sidnomwende and his family make Sagabo and Okra Sauce, a meal from Burkina Faso. Here is the correct sequence and some useful information for you to help your child/ren to understand what it takes to grow and prepare a meal.

PRAYER POINT
Pray for Tearfund and people in countries like Burkina Faso who are working together to find innovative ways to overcome food shortages. Visit www.tearfund.org for stories of Tearfund's partners.

Devotion 5

MONEY OX

AIM: To begin to consider our response to people who have no or little food.

What you ought to know

The UN Food and Agriculture Organisation classifies 87 countries as low-income food-deficit countries that can't grow enough to feed their people and lack the wealth to make up the deficit with imports. Almost half of these (41) are in sub-Saharan Africa. Local changes in the climate in some parts of Ethiopia have shortened the rainy seasons and caused crops to fail. Some areas have had very little rain for the past three years. Many Ethiopians who, like the people of Burkina Faso, rely on livestock for farming have had to sell their oxen at low prices because they can't afford to feed them or their families.

In 2005 the number of people in urgent need of food aid was almost nine million. Tearfund partners like the Ethiopian Full Gospel Believers Church (FGBC) are able to respond to food crises with the support of Tearfund's Disaster Management Teams. FGBC run a supplementary feeding programme, reaching more than 10,000 children and 1000 nursing mothers. As they distribute food, FGBC teach mothers more about nutrition and health. They also run projects which hopefully will help communities to be better equipped to avoid future food shortages, teaching them better farming practices and improved irrigation methods.

Governments need to take seriously their responsibility to ensure everyone has adequate access, either to grow food or to buy the food they need. Supply of food needs to be stable, in terms of production, distribution and price. Economic, as well as political, instability tends to mean people become dependent on food aid. If people in poor countries are ever to overcome their food shortages or reliance on emergency aid, more investment is needed in long-term development. If we're prepared to do something about it ourselves, we are in a better position to be able to challenge our governments to increase their investment in poorer communities. We've already seen how something as simple as training, tools and resources like a cow can make a real difference to people's abilities to feed themselves and their families.

What your family could do

Introduction: Use the 'Money Ox' to think about how much your daily food relies on cows. Place it somewhere visible in your kitchen and use it to keep count. Convert your ticks into coins.

You will need: *Printable 5: Money Ox* (CD-ROM)

Print off and make up the 'Money Ox'. The card from a used cereal box is the ideal thickness to use to make your box.

Every time you eat, cook or use foods that are dairy products – milk, butter, cheese, etc. – record this on the ox using a tick or tally chart.

Also mark the ox every time you use something that would need, in a poor country, a cow or ox in order to make it grow, i.e. food that requires ploughing or fertilizer, such as cornflakes or sweetcorn.

Every week, count up your ticks and convert them to coins.

Once you feel you've collected what you can, send your gift to Tearfund in order to help them to provide more assistance to projects like the ones operating in Ethiopia and Burkina Faso, who amongst other things provide food and ways to access food in the places that need it most.

> **PRAYER POINT**
> The actual cost of oxen fluctuates. Under drought conditions prices are low, whereas when there is plenty of grazing land people will hang on to their cattle and keep prices high.
> - £75 is approximately how much it would cost to buy someone an ox in countries like Ethiopia or Burkina Faso.
> - It may sound a like lot, but that's less than £1.50 a week for one year.
>
> Pray about ways you could encourage your class at school or other families in your street or church to get involved.

Devotion 6

JESUS FEEDS THE FIVE THOUSAND

AIM: To develop an understanding of Jesus' desire to provide for people's basic needs. To apply Jesus' model of how to serve others to our lives.

What you ought to know

Every year there is a global surplus of crops such as grain, corn, rice and sorghum. Despite the fact that this figure stands at somewhere around 300 million tonnes, over 800 million people in the world are hungry and 20 per cent of people worldwide are still undernourished.[46] People all over the world are going hungry, not necessarily because there is a shortage of food but because they can't always access it – either they are too poor to afford it or they have no land to grow it.

Jesus' feeding of the five thousand is a great example of how he's concerned about meeting people's needs, not just spiritually but physically too. In Matthew's account of the event he describes how everyone was satisfied; they all had enough – not too little or too much, but enough. When the disciples had finished serving the people there were twelve basketfuls of food left, but even the leftovers were not wasted – as John 6:12 says 'Let nothing be wasted.' Those of us that have food are often terribly wasteful with what we have and we don't think of others who don't.

Why Matthew feels he has to mention 12 baskets of leftovers is unclear. Perhaps there was one for each of the 12 disciples. Maybe there is something significant here about the fact that even if we put the needs of others before ours, our needs, not wants, will be taken care of too. God wants everyone to have enough food to eat. There is enough food in the world for everyone. We, like the disciples, need to serve people. It is not just in poor countries that people go to bed hungry, it happens in our communities. Perhaps God is asking you to get involved in a project that is working with the hungry. We need to seek what God is asking us to do.

What your family could do

Introduction: Read together the story of when Jesus feeds the five thousand (Mt. 14:13-21). Specifically consider verses 18-20:

> Jesus said, 'Bring me the bread and the fish to me.' Then he told the people to sit down on the grass. He took the five loaves of bread and the two fish. Then he looked to heaven and thanked God for the food. Jesus divided the loaves of bread. He gave them to his followers, and they gave the bread to the people. All the people ate and were satisfied. After they finished eating, the followers filled 12 baskets with the pieces of food that were not eaten.[47]

You will need: a children's Bible: for younger children try Lois Rock's *A Little Life of Jesus* (p. 123), published by Lion Hudson; for older children try the *International Children's Bible*, published by Authentic Media.

Key questions to discuss as a family:
- What are the different ways that Jesus shows he cares for people in the parable?
- Why do you think the disciples responded to Jesus as they did when he suggested they feed the crowd?
- Why did Jesus think it was important the crowd weren't sent away to eat?
- What did Jesus do with the small amount of food before he shared it out?
- What should you remember to do before you eat? Why?
- In what ways would the crowds thinking about God have been affected by Jesus' idea to share the food?

- In what ways do you think you might serve the people you know in the same way the disciples did?
- Do you know people who don't have much food? What do you think you could do?

PRAYER POINT
Pray for people who don't have much food and make a commitment to God to do whatever you can to enable them to access it.

Devotion 7

WASTE NOT, WANT NOT

AIM: To identify how to use food responsibly.

What you ought to know

In the UK 3220 tonnes of edible food goes unsold every year.[48] The average British adult throws away £420 worth of food annually.[49] Despite the fact that there is enough food in the world for everyone, all over the world people are not getting enough to eat – children and families just like yours. Fairtrade food, something we'll consider in Chapter 5, is one way we can directly help to support agriculture and food production through our purchases, but for now we'll focus on utilizing the potential of all the food we waste. It has been reported that in total Britain throws away £20 billion worth of unused food every year – equal to five times our spending on international aid and enough to lift 150 million people out of starvation.[50] We can't exactly send it overseas but we can do something with the food we usually waste to help people 'over here'.

You may not realize it, but there are currently 4 million people in this country who do not have enough to eat. Some supermarkets and local charities have introduced schemes to offer food to local people and projects. A charity called FareShare supplies 12,000 meals a day to homeless and vulnerable people, using surplus food provided by supermarkets. There are eight FareShare schemes operating in partnership with local charities across the UK, working in partnership with over 150 companies and 250 local charities. In 2004, FareShare distributed 1800 tonnes of quality food that would normally go to landfill. This surplus food contributes to over 2.5 million meals for people in need. FareShare found that 60 per cent of the projects they serve could now spend money in other areas such as training, medical services and counselling, which help people to start rebuilding their lives. Now 84 per cent of these projects can regularly provide a wider range of healthier food.

What your family could do

Introduction: Think about how you could make changes to prevent food waste which could benefit your family and the families of others.

The next time food is left over after a meal, take the time to discuss why there is food left and what you could do with it. Perhaps you could freeze your leftovers or recycle leftovers by using them on the garden.[51] Also discuss why you may throw food away – perhaps because it is out of date or going mouldy. As a family, you could consider buying less but more often and buying locally as and when you need it. Explain that we need to value the food we have and learn to use it responsibly.

If you'd like to make a change locally, why not find out if there are similar projects to FareShare near you. If so join them; if not see if it's a need in your area that you could begin to address. Visit www.fareshare.org.uk for more information.

HELPFUL HINT

Express Community is a resource designed to enable small groups to better meet the needs of their local community. You may find some of the sessions and exercises it contains useful in discovering what the issues within your community really are. Published by Authentic Media, it is available from Tearfund (0845 355 8355), local Christian bookshops or www.wesleyowen.com priced at £7.99 (ISBN 185078583X).

Feeding people who are short of food is not as simple as sending food overseas yourself. So what can we do? Why don't you go without snacks, such as sweets, lollies or chocolate, for a week? Collect what you save and send it to Tearfund to help families in countries like Ethiopia and Burkina Faso to be better equipped to avoid food shortages (use *Printable 5: Money Ox* from the CD-ROM).

And/or

Check out your family food bill before and after you implement any lifestyle changes. If you find that as a family you are beginning to save money, thank God and make an offering of the money to Tearfund so that they can support projects serving people with little or no food.

> **PRAYER POINT**
> Thank God for the food you have, pray about the ways you've thought about wasting less food and ask him to help you to make better use of food that would otherwise get wasted.

4 Shopping for Clothes

What follows is a series of devotions designed to enable your family to connect with the issues of clothing, garment workers and God's heart for the poor. Choose as many or as few as seems appropriate to your context. Most of us, and children in particular, learn best by doing, so whilst some are reflective, the majority of these activities are practical. It is important that all family members are involved, not just the children, as actions that develop thinking and change habits are about learning together and from one another.

Your devotions on shopping for clothes will help you to:

1 identify where clothes are made
2 understand the working conditions of some of the people who make our clothes
3 work out how little people tend to get paid for the clothes we wear
4 think about how the money we spend on clothes is spent and whether we feel it's fair
5 understand how Jesus' actions made a real difference to people who acted unjustly
6 think about how you would like the people who make your clothes to be treated
7 think about your spending and how you can make a difference.

Your way in

Everyday situations that your child/ren might face, or natural conversations that you might have as a family, will provide some of the best ways in to exploring the issue of clothes shopping and the poor. Look out for things your child/ren say and do as they begin to widen their perspective of their whole wide world and use these as a stimulus or way in to the subject in question.

Shopping for Clothes

WHAT YOUR CHILD/REN MIGHT...

DO	SAY
Shop for clothes	'I don't like this any more.'
Mistreat their clothes	'None of my friends wear these anymore.'
Ruin their 'best' clothes	
Refuse to wear certain clothes	'I really need that new pair of trainers.'
Be fussy about what they wear	'So who makes my clothes?'
Moan about the clothes you buy them	'What do children my age do during the day?'
Want what their friends have	'Why are some children treated so badly?'
	'What can we do about it?'
Hate clothes shopping	'So what can we buy?'
Love clothes shopping	'Where can we shop?'
Watch adverts	'Should we stop buying clothes?'

Devotion 1

WHERE DO CLOTHES COME FROM?

AIM: To identify where clothes are made. To begin to consider how the people who make our clothes are treated.

What you ought to know

Before you try on your next jeans or new coat, stop and think about how much the people behind your potential purchase were paid, how many hours they worked or what kind of conditions they worked in. Many of the people who provide our clothes live in the world's poorest countries, working long hours in unsafe and unhealthy conditions. Eight hundred and fifty million people worldwide are employed on less than a living wage, which means they can't feed their families or pay for medicine when they get ill and can't afford to live in what we would class as below

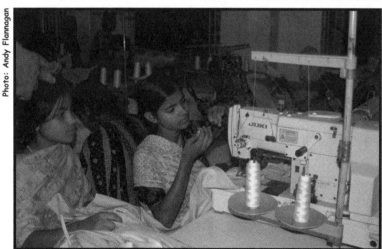

Shima started working in a garment factory when she was just fourteen years old. She works 8am to 9pm, six days a week, earning just £4.00 a week.

average accommodation.[52] Two hundred and fifty million of these workers are children, who, instead of going to school, have to sit and make clothes day in day out, week in week out, year in year out.[53] Jesus told his disciples to clothe the poor (Mt. 25: 31-46), but it seems it's the poor who are clothing us.

Shima left school when she was thirteen, even though she wanted to stay on. She was too poor to study and her family needed what little money she could earn to help them all survive. Shima left home and moved to Bangladesh's capital city, Dhaka, and for three years she has been making button holes in jeans and jackets 13 hours a day, six days a week in a hot factory that has no fans. For her time she gets 1700 taka (about £20) per month. She spends a third of it on rent, and even then she can only afford to live in a slum. As Shima says: 'This wage is not enough to live on.'

It's not even enough to stay safe on. The slums are a dangerous place for women and girls like Shima to be at night; theft and rape are common. Thirty-one garment workers were raped in the space of one month as they walked home late at night from the factories – they were too poorly paid to use public transport.

What your family could do

Introduction: Look at where clothes are made and start to consider how people who make our clothes are treated.

You will need: clothes, *Printable 6: Washing instructions* (CD-ROM), *Map of the world* (Poster Pack), paper, drawing materials, *Photograph 7* (Poster Pack/CD-ROM)

Gather together a selection of clothes from your family's wardrobes and find out the different countries they were made in by looking at the labels. Find the countries they come from on the map.

Print off *Printable 6: Washing instructions* and ask your children if they can guess what each symbol means. Now look at the labels on your clothes and think about how they tell you to care for the clothes. What is missing from the label? What aren't we told? (Basically, how the workers who made them are cared for.)

PRAYER POINT

Use *Photograph 7*, which features Shima, to help explain to your child/ren some of the conditions other children work in. Use the points below as a structure for your discussion/prayers.

- Shima left school at 13, even though she wanted to stay at school.
- Shima's family needed her to earn money to help them all survive.
- Shima has left her home and moved to Bangladesh's capital city, Dhaka.
- She makes button holes in jeans and jackets.
- She works 13 hours a day, six days a week in a hot factory that has no fans.
- She gets paid £20 a month.

Pray for the people who make our clothes – that they will be treated fairly.

Shopping for Clothes

Devotion 2

WHERE DOES MY MONEY GO?

AIM: To think about how the money we spend on clothes is spent and whether we feel it's fair.

What you ought to know

The Clean Clothes Campaign, a European and International network of organizations campaigning to improve workers pay, conditions and rights in the garment industry, recently calculated the price breakdown on an average pair of trainers. Out of the final selling price of £60:

- the retailer got 50 per cent
- the brand name 33 per cent
- transport cost 5 per cent
- the factory that produced it got 12 per cent
- the worker less than 0.4 per cent.[54]

The pressure placed on workers like Shima (Devotion 1) by their employers must be immense, but even they have their reasons. Factories often struggle to meet the demands of multinational and UK companies for cheaper and faster fashion. Factories are often under pressure to meet unrealistic deadlines; if they fail they face the very real prospect of losing a valuable contract. They may have to employ more workers to work longer hours but for less money.

But hard labour is not entirely the clothing company's fault; some of the unfairness suffered by the people who make our clothing rests on our shoulders. Whether you choose to browse the high street or the web, prices are competitive because we all like a good bargain. We have money and we choose where to spend it. Shops know that if their stock is 'right now' and at the 'right price' we'll buy it. Our pressure, high street pressure and factory floor pressure all leads somewhere. The workers pay the real price for our fashion. They work harder, faster and for less so that we can get more, quicker and cheaper.

What your family could do

Introduction: Before you consider what to do in response to low wages think about how unfairly the price you pay for clothing is divided up.

You will need: paper, scissors, pens, a trainer

Draw around a trainer. Explain how the price we pay for a pair of trainers is split between:

- the shop – 50 per cent (a huge slice goes to the retailer, which more than covers its overheads)
- the brand – 33 per cent (to cover its marketing and other overheads, with the rest making up the profit)
- the factory – 12 per cent (to pay for premises and wages of employees)
- transport – 5 per cent (these companies make money by making sure that the garments get to the shops on time)
- the workers – 0.4 per cent (you'll see that on a £30 pair of trainers it's not much of a wage at all).

Split the outline of your trainer into parts appropriately as you explain this (see the diagram overleaf).

> **PRAYER POINT**
> Discuss what you feel about this and then turn over your template and divide the trainer up, either by drawing or cutting the pattern into what you feel would be a fairer way to divide up the money. Label each piece and pray together for each of these areas.

Shopping for Clothes

Illustration: Andy Baldwin

WHO GETS WHAT?

50% THE SHOP
33% THE BRAND
12% THE FACTORY
5% TRANSPORT
0.4% THE WORKER

Devotion 3

CLOTHES CALCULATOR

AIM: To work out how much people tend to get paid for the clothes we wear.

What you ought to know

The Clean Clothes Campaign suggests that millions of garment workers around the world are paid well below their country's national minimum wage. On average, workers' wages are less than 0.5 per cent of the price you pay.[55] For every pair of trainers you buy at £50, or for every £50 jacket, the person can expect to get just 25p. Mexico, a country whose president once boasted had 'labour costs that are some of lowest in the world', has a legal minimum wage that is only 25 per cent of what a family of four needs to live on.[56] The cost of living is obviously lower in a poorer country than ours, therefore you'd expect wages to be less. However, what's in doubt here is not whether people's pay is equivalent to ours but whether it's enough to live on.

- **What people are paid**: In El Salvador, women sewing garments for a major sportswear company are working eight hours a day for just £2.87.
- **What people need**: They need 41 pence for their bus fare to and from work, 48 pence for a basic breakfast, 89 pence for lunch (both of which they are forced to buy from their employer's canteen).
- **What's left**: With the remaining £1.09, they need to find 62 pence per day to rent a ten by twelve foot room and at least 60 pence to provide supper for a family of three.[57]

Do the maths and you'll realize that even without the additional cost of childcare or the clothes they need to buy, they're way short. Who knows what might happen if they were ever to get ill. What kind of a future do they have whilst they work these kinds of hours, earning this kind of money, and living that kind of life? Workers being paid more doesn't mean you'll have to pay lots more. Workers in Thailand calculated that in order to double what they were paid for each pair of trainers it would cost you the equivalent of a pair of laces.[58]

What your family could do

Introduction: Work out what people tend to get paid for the clothes they make for us.

You will need: *Interactive 1: Clothes calculator* (CD-ROM open with Internet Explorer), paper, drawing materials

Each member of your family needs to draw a picture of themselves wearing their favourite outfit. Label how much each item costs, then work out the cost in total of their outfit. Take a guess at what you feel the workers' wages for this outfit would have been. Get other family members to say whether they think it's higher or lower. In turn, enter the total cost of each outfit into the 'Clothes calculator'.

See what the workers would have got

- How does this make you feel?
- What could you buy for that kind of money?
- Explain that people can't live on that kind of money.

> **PRAYER POINT**
> Pray about how you can make the way you spend your money count. Put pressure on our high street shops to deliver better wages.

Boycotting companies will only further reduce the wages people receive, so unless there is an ethical or Fairtrade alternative; it's better to continue to shop where we do but to ask questions and to put pressure on companies to treat people fairly. (We'll think more about the right questions to ask in Devotion 7.)

Devotion 4

SEEING THE PEOPLE BEHIND THE PRODUCTS

AIM: To understand the working conditions of some of the people who make our clothes.

What you ought to know

Rokye sits crossed legged on a long bench, just one of many workers who sit hunched over denim jackets, each repeating exactly the same action. They are working on a jacket dubbed the '315' jacket – each one has 315 diamante beads sewn on it, by hand, one by one. Each bead is so small that Rokye holds the material close to his eyes, straining to thread the bead. His fingernails are yellow at the tips, bruised from the needles.

He is not allowed to talk as he works. Workers sit in silence and only talk when spoken to by managers – workers can be fined for talking. Rokye normally works 8 a.m. to 8 p.m., although he says, 'Often I work a double shift until 2 a.m. or 3 a.m., with one break.'

Often cheques are not paid on time or workers have to wait up to two months to receive wages. Rokye, and his fellow workers, can expect to work 15 hours a day, six or even seven days a week, all for just £4. That's an incredible 60p a day, 4p an hour! Rokye rents a room in a Dhaka slum, sharing a small cramped space with five others. There are open sewers and no electricity. Clean water is available, but most garment industry workers cannot afford it. Disease is rife. The factory that Rokye works in produces a staggering 15,000 items of clothes every day. It's one of 3,024 factories in Bangladesh employing over 1.5 million people,[59] some of them with similar stories to Rokye, and supplying clothes to stores that we visit regularly.

Shopping for Clothes

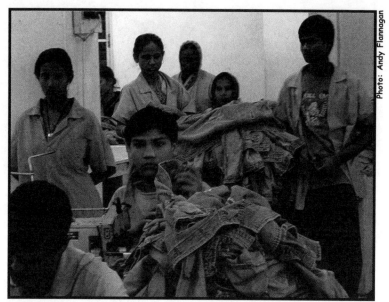

A fellow garment worker in Rokye's factory, Dhaka, Bangladesh.

What your family could do

Introduction: Use a video to stimulate discussion about how the people who make our clothes should be treated.

You will need: *Video 1: Lift the Label* (CD-ROM)

Watch the video and use the following discussion points to think about conditions of workers.

- Why do you think Royke's fingernails were yellow at the tips and bruised?
- How would you feel about sowing 315 tiny beads on by hand, one by one?
- Rokye can't talk when he's at work. How does it make you feel when you're told not to talk?
- Rokye doesn't always get paid on time. How do you think that would feel? What effect would that have? What might he need money for?

- Rokye earns just 60p a day – what sort of things would you normally buy with 60p?
- Rokye lives in one room and shares this with five other people. How do you think he feels about this?
- Rokye doesn't have any electricity and can't afford to buy clean water. What effects do you think this has on his life?

PRAYER POINT
Pray for the people who've handled your clothes before you put them on each morning.

Devotion 5

THE STORY OF ZACCHAEUS

AIM: To show how Jesus' decision to go against the feelings of the crowd and to speak to one man who had power and money made a real difference to lots of others.

What you ought to know

The story of Zacchaeus is well known. He was a tax collector who cheated people. As a result of this he was not liked by other people and people didn't want anything to do with him. But Jesus noticed him; Jesus went and spent time with him. From spending time with Jesus, Zacchaeus more than repaid the people he had cheated. Why did Zacchaeus change in this way?

Jesus didn't avoid awkward situations: he knew what needed to be done and did it. We need to be more like Jesus: we need to take action and make sure that the people behind the products we buy are paid and treated fairly. We need to start talking to the people in power, those with the money, making the decisions with our shopping, rather than avoiding them because they make us feel uncomfortable or we don't like what they do. We need to be standing up for what is just.

Zacchaeus' response to the love Jesus showed him was to reject the unjust tax system imposed by the Romans. What is our response to Jesus' love to us, to accept or reject how people are treated by the 'system'? How do you think clothing manufacturers will respond to Jesus' love demonstrated through your willingness to engage with them?

What your family could do

Introduction: Read together the story of Zacchaeus the Tax Collector (Lk. 19:1-8). Specifically consider verses 5-7:

When Jesus came to that place [the tree Zacchaeus had climbed], he looked up and saw Zacchaeus in the tree. He said to him, 'Zacchaeus, hurry and come down! I must stay at your house today.' Zacchaeus came down quickly. He was pleased to have Jesus in his house. All the people saw this and began to complain, 'Look at the kind of man Jesus stays with. Zacchaeus is a sinner!' But Zacchaeus said to the Lord, 'I will give half of my money to the poor. If I have cheated anyone, I will pay that person back four times more.' [60]

You will need: A children's Bible: for younger children try Nick Butterworth and Mick Inkpen's *The Magpie's Tale – Jesus and Zacchaeus*, published by Marshall Pickering; for older children try the *International Children's Bible*, published by Authentic Media.

Key questions to discuss as a family:
- Why was Zacchaeus so rich?
- Why did Jesus spend time with him?
- Why did other people think it was such a bad idea?
- What effect did Jesus spending time with one man have?
- Why on this occasion didn't Jesus choose to spend time with the whole crowd?
- Discuss any people you know who are mistreating others because they have money, power or influence. What do you think Jesus would have to say to them?

PRAYER POINT
Ask God to place people around those who have the power and influence to make a difference to the thousands of garment workers who are cheated out of wages that are rightfully theirs. Pray they will begin to use our money more wisely.

Devotion 6

SEEMS FAIR TO ME

AIM: To help children to think about how they would like the people who make their clothes to be treated.

What you ought to know

People Tree works with 70 Fairtrade groups in 20 countries, giving design and technical assistance to marginalized producers struggling to sell their products. People Tree pays a fair price, gives advance credit when needed and commits to ordering regularly. Director Safia Miney is frustrated at the way fashion buyers seem to be more interested in quality and production deadlines than in salary or working conditions. She'd like to see more of the UK clothing industry signing up to the Ethical Trading Initiative (ETI), an alliance of companies, non-governmental organizations and trade unions that identifies and promotes good practice through the implementation of its codes of labour practice:

- Employment is freely chosen.[61]
- Freedom of association and the right to collective bargaining.[62]
- Working conditions are safe and hygienic.[63]
- Child labour shall not be used.[64]
- Working hours are not excessive.[65]
- No discrimination.[66]
- Regular employment is provided.[67]
- No harsh or inhumane treatment is allowed.[68]
- Living wages are paid.[69]

The ETI has one of the best codes of conduct, which companies can use as their own code. It offers a limited first step on the way to a more ethical way of trading clothes, one which proper legislation would ensure. ETI's members want to ensure that the working conditions of workers in companies that supply goods to consumers in the UK meet international standards. Some guidelines are better than no guidelines, but since the ETI's guidelines are voluntary, companies can chose to abide by them or not. Signing a code of conduct is one thing; carrying out what it says is another. Safia Minney is keen to see is that: 'The bare minimum for the high street is for manufacturers and retailers to implement properly the Ethical Trade Initiative.'

What your family could do

Introduction: Write your own family guidelines for how you'd like the people who make your clothes to be treated.

You will need: Pens, pencils, paper, *Printable 7: T-shirt* (CD-ROM)

Several leading companies are members of the Ethical Trading Initiative – including Sainsbury's, Levi Strauss, Marks & Spencer, Monsoon and Tesco. Their aim is to work towards ensuring that all the clothes they sell are made by workers who enjoy fair working conditions as laid down in the ETI's code of practice. The ETI's 'Base Code' calls for safe, hygienic factories, collective bargaining, fair pay, an end to child labour, living wages, reasonable working hours and regular employment.

Print off the T-shirt and on it write your family's checklist of how you'd like to feel the people who make your clothes are being treated. For example:

- 'I would like children not to have to work.'
- 'I would like people to be able to work normal hours.'

PRAYER POINT

Before you consider your response to clothes shopping with your child, think through the Ethical Trading Initiative (ETI) code of conduct for yourself.

Discuss and then pray about creative ways that you and your family could begin to change the way high street shops provide our clothes.

Devotion 7

WHAT WE OUGHT TO WEAR

AIM: To think about what you could do to ensure the clothes you wear are made fairly.

What you ought to know

UK shoppers spend an incredible £30 billion a year on clothes. Of that, £18 billion is spent on womenswear, £8.8 on menswear and over £6 billion on childrenswear.[70] With that kind of spending power, don't you think we have the right to question how our garments are made? Don't you think clothes companies will listen? Some do, and are prepared to put good practice before profits. Members of the ETI are committed to adopting the standards that are contained in the ETI Base Code. They can either adopt the base code as their own, or take some of the relevant standards and put them into their own code. The Ethical Trading Initiative Base Code is better than many codes, as it includes standards taken from the relevant International Labour Organisation (ILO), the UN agency that seeks the promotion of social justice and internationally recognized human and labour rights. The ETI code is not enforceable. Purchasing a product from a shop that has signed up to the ETI won't guarantee that you're buying goods produced under the nine conditions listed in Devotion 6, but that the company has made an agreement to work towards them.

What is important is to ensure you are informed about the places you choose to make your fashion statements. By visiting clothing company websites you should find details of their ethical policies or codes of conducts. The Good Shopping Guide is a leading ethical reference guide listing the ethical level of companies behind hundreds of everyday consumer brands. The Good Shopping Guide Logo shows that a brand has scored well when ethically tested on human rights, animal welfare and care of the environment. Ethical Consumer magazine provides up-to-date information on high street company policies and practices. As well as clothes shops, you can find buyers' guides on baby buggies and car seats, cars, computers, fridges and freezers, furniture shops, mobile phones, paint, tissues, toothpaste, TVs, vacuum cleaners and even washing up liquid. Visit their website at www.ethicalconsumer.org for back issues of buyer guides.

> **HELPFUL HINT**
> Ethiscore is Ethical Consumer's new online shopping guide. You can check out their most recent reports on different products like chocolate, trainers and internet banks. Visit www.ethiscore.org for more details.

What your family could do

Introduction: When we shop, it's important that we don't shop quietly, but instead encourage high street shops, manufacturers and retailers to first sign up and then to fully implement the ETI guidelines

You will need: Your checklist from Devotion 6.

Next time you go clothes shopping together, encourage your child/ren to use the checklist you have made as a family (see Devotion 6) to ensure their purchases were made fairly. Discuss as a family the kind of questions you'd like to ask the people who sell the clothes you wear and that others make.

> **HELPFUL HINT**
> When possible try to fill in customer comment cards. Explain that you would like a written response. Write the following questions on them and hand them to the manager asking them to pass them on to the company's CEO (Chief Executive).

Shopping for Clothes

- Where are your clothes made?
- What steps are you taking to ensure that people making your clothes work in safe and healthy conditions and are paid a fair wage they can live on?
- Is your company a member of the Ethical Trading Initiative?

Just as the Fairtrade Mark ensures us that, amongst other things, the food that reaches our table has done so fairly – something we'll consider in the next chapter – the labels we wear should say just as much about how we care for the person who made them as they do about how to care for the clothes themselves.

PRAYER POINT
Before you shop, don't forget to pray about the people behind your products and make a commitment to speak up on their behalf.

5 Shopping for Food

What follows is a series of devotions designed to enable your family to connect with the issues of eating, growing, food production and God's heart for the poor. Choose as many or as few as seems appropriate to your context. Most of us, and children in particular, learn best by doing, so whilst some are reflective, the majority of these activities are practical. It is important that all family members are involved, not just the children, as actions that develop thinking and change habits are about learning together and from one another.

Your devotions on shopping for food will help you to:

1 understand where foods come from
2 understand the difference we can make by buying products that have the Fairtrade Mark
3 identify products that are made fairly
4 understand the effects of buying these products on the people who grow the food
5 enjoy using Fairtrade products
6 consider different ways of sharing your understanding of the benefits of buying fairly traded products
7 provide an opportunity to reflect on what your children have learnt about Fairtrade and/or ethical clothing.

Your way in

Everyday situations that your child/ren might face, or natural conversations that you might have as a family, will provide some of the best ways in to exploring the issue of food shopping and the poor. Look out for things your child/ren say and do as they begin to widen their perspective of their whole wide world and use these as a stimulus or way in to the subject in question.

Shopping for Food

WHAT YOUR CHILD/REN MIGHT...

DO	SAY
Never thought about the people who grow most of our food	'Where does our food come from?'
Enjoy helping you food shop	'What do the people who grow our food get paid?'
Hate helping you food shop	'Does it really matter what type of food we buy?'
Put food they want in the shopping trolley	'How can we make sure people get paid fairly?'
Have pocket money which they can spend on food treats	'What is Fairtrade?'
	'How do we know something is Fairtrade?'
Ask why you buy certain brands	'Fairtrade is unfair because there's not enough choice.'
Enjoy baking	
Enjoy picnics	'...it's unfair because it only benefits a few.'
Want to share what they are learning about the poor with their friends	'Fairtrade costs too much money.'
Think about the kind of jobs people around the world do	'Can we buy anything else which is fairly traded?'

Devotion 1

WHERE DOES FOOD COME FROM?

AIM: To develop a knowledge and understanding of where foods come from. To highlight areas of the world where people aren't paid fairly for the work they do.

What you ought to know

Whether you're up-to-date with your child's latest playground craze, into sharing the 'odd' item of clothing with friends, or enjoy browsing the sales of this century at a popular online auction site, you ought to be aware that buying and selling impacts the lives of billions of people daily. The fuel in our cars, the flex in our kettle and the food on our plates are all global contributions to our lives. Martin Luther King once said that, 'before you sit down to breakfast you will have relied on half the world'.

In fact whether you had a juice, an espresso or grapefruit for breakfast this morning, the average distance it will have travelled in order to reach you will be an incredible 5000 miles.[71] So do you ever start your day by considering the real impact of your food?

In the last forty years the prices paid for much of the food we rely on, produced in warmer climates, have plummeted. The cost of fertilizers, pesticides and machinery those countries import from richer countries however, have shot up. When the market price of commodities drops below the cost of production, people in poor countries have to work harder and longer for less money. In the 1990s millions of overseas farmers found themselves in debt and lost their land as a result of the low prices they received for crops like coffee.

What your family could do

Introduction: Look at the areas of the world where certain types of food come from.

You will need: *Map of the world* (Poster Pack), *Printable 8: Food and drink* (CD-ROM).

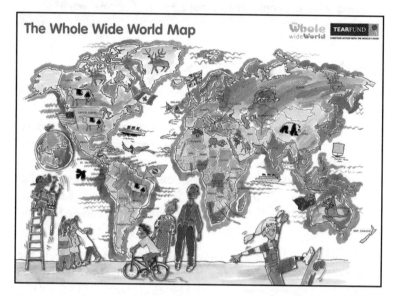

Ask your child/ren to think about what they had for breakfast this morning and to think about where it may have come from. Whether they realize it or not, their breakfast will have travelled half way around the world! Using a map of the world, get children to put pictures of food and drink on some of the countries that those items come from. Refer to the table opposite for guidance.

Food	Country it came from
Bananas	India, Ecuador, Brazil, China, Costa Rica, Mexico, Thailand, Colombia.[72]
Cocoa (used to make chocolate)	Ghana, Brazil, Venezuela, Mexico, Nicaragua, Guatemala, Colombia.
Coffee	Colombia, Ethiopia, Costa Rica, Honduras, Kenya, Nicaragua, Peru, Tanzania, Bolivia, Mexico.
Honey	Argentina, Australia, Canada, United States, Chile, Nicaragua.
Oranges	Brazil.
Sugar	Costa Rica.[73]
Tea	China, India, Tanzania.

This activity highlights the parts of the world where people aren't always paid fairly for the work they do.

PRAYER POINT

Use the map and pray for each of the countries that have food on them. Write prayers on your pictures of food and drink; thank God for the people who grow them and ask him that they would be paid fairly.

Shopping for Food

Devotion 2

FOOD TASTING

AIM: To develop an understanding of the difference we can make by buying products that have the Fairtrade Mark.

What you ought to know

Rosa is one of 120,000 small-scale coffee farmers in Peru who are struggling to make a living from the crop that once promised them a route out of poverty. A mother of six, she is dependent on her income from coffee. The price she receives is a third of what it used to be. It's barely enough to live on, but she's out of options. Middlemen purchase her coffee and form the first link in the long and complex commercial chain between producer (her) and consumer (you and me). Rosa says: 'Whatever price the buyer offers, I have to accept.'

Buyers all agree the price beforehand. She can't sell direct to companies as they only buy from middlemen. In contrast Pedro, who is also a coffee farmer from Peru, is a member of a cooperative called Bagua Grande. They sell 30 per cent of their coffee to the Fairtrade market, mostly Cafédirect, for more than double the conventional market price. Farmers who are part of Bagua Grande agree the prices together. The cooperative director says: 'the price we get on the international market doesn't compensate for the work we put in. Our hope is in the Fairtrade market.'

Higher prices mean greater investment in homes and education, access to business management training and advice on how to improve crop quality. It even funds health insurance schemes.

What your family could do

Introduction: Compare how Fairtrade and non-Fairtrade food taste.

You will need: blindfolds, bananas, chocolate, juice, biscuits, *Photograph 8* (Poster Pack/CD-ROM)

Set up a taste test using blindfolds and the following food and drink:
• bananas • chocolate • juice • biscuits.

Remember to include Fairtrade and non-Fairtrade foods. See how difficult it is to tell which is which. You and your child/ren probably won't taste any difference. Fairtrade food is no way an inferior product compared to the better known brands. Emphasize that they need to look for the Fairtrade Mark when they shop. Explain that even if they don't taste the difference the workers get treated differently – they get treated fairly.

PRAYER POINT

Share the story of Rosa and Pedro. If it helps, summarize their contrasting stories using the following basic points:

• Rosa and her six children live in Peru in South America.

• Rosa grows coffee, but finds it hard to live on the money she gets for it because the price is now a third less than it used to be.

• The people who buy Rosa's coffee decide the price they want to pay her for it; she has no choice but to sell it to them.

• Unlike Rosa, other coffee farmers in Peru, farmers like Pedro, can decide the price they get paid for their coffee because it's Fairtrade.

• Pedro gets double the price people like Rosa get. With the money Pedro earns he can improve his home, receive education and pay for medicine when he gets sick.

Using *Photograph 8*, pray for Rosa and farmers like her.

Devotion 3

FAIRTRADE HUNT

AIMS: To identify products that are made fairly. To begin to consider the effects of buying these products on the people who produce the foods.

What you ought to know

In the 1990s development agencies were quick to recognize the important role consumers could play in helping producers to find ways to escape the poverty caused by the fall in prices paid for their crops. By buying direct from farmers at better prices and marketing their produce directly through shops and catalogues, charities were able to offer consumers the opportunity to buy products bought on the basis of fair trade. Hundreds of small poor farmers were able to get back on their feet and trade their way out of poverty. The Fairtrade Mark now exists to guarantee:

- farmer organizations receive a fair and stable price for their products
- extra income for farmers and plantation workers to improve their lives
- greater respect for the environment
- small farmers a stronger position in world markets
- a closer link between consumer and producers.

The Fairtrade Foundation is the organization that is responsible for assessing and monitoring whether a company is suitable to be awarded the Fairtrade Mark. It promotes Fairtrade as an idea and generates greater sales.

Tesco and Co-op both stock Fairtrade Oranges and Pineapples, and along with Sainsbury's, Waitrose, Safeway, Asda, Somerfield and Budgens, they also stock Fairtrade bananas.

Fairtrade coffee and tea is available from most major supermarkets, many of which now have their own brand. Fairtrade sugar is available at Tesco, Budgens and Co-op. Sainsbury's, Tesco, Asda, Somerfield, Safeway, Waitrose and Co-op all stock Fairtrade juice. All Co-op's own brand of chocolate is Fairtrade. In addition to food, Tesco also sells Fairtrade roses.

What your family could do

Introduction: Set your child/ren the task of finding as many products as they can which display the Fairtrade Mark. Either let them find Fairtrade food you already buy in your cupboards, or take a trip to the supermarket to see what Fairtrade food is available there.

You will need: clipboard, pen/pencil, *Printable 9: Fairtrade Mark* (CD-ROM)

You will need to provide each child with a clipboard and a pen to either draw or write down the foods they find. On the top of their piece of paper it would be useful to put a copy of the Fairtrade Mark so they know what they are looking for.

Afterwards, take the time to discuss, if you haven't already done so, why products have the Fairtrade Mark and the difference buying Fairtrade products makes to the workers – that they receive a fair and stable price for their products.

PRAYER POINT
Discuss what a difference it would make to you as a family to buy Fairtrade products. Thank God that we can buy products that we know guarantee the workers a fair wage.

Devotion 4

FAIRTRADE RECIPE

AIM: To enjoy using Fairtrade food products to make banana splits.

What you ought to know

Forty-three year old Nioka is one of 605 small farmers (many of whom are women) now registered with The Windward Islands Farmers Association. Nioka has been growing bananas on a two-acre plot (leased from the government) in the north of St Vincent for thirteen years. For the last two years, Nioka has been selling bananas to the Fairtrade market and is now the chairperson of the local Fairtrade group in the small community of Langley Park.

Nioka is a banana farmer from the Windward Islands. Bananas are her livelihood.

Banana growing is physically demanding and often tedious work, but for women like Nioka – a single parent with four sons aged between nine and twenty-six – it's her only real means of earning a decent living.

'Bananas are my livelihood,' says Nioka. 'They are what help me meet the needs of my family.'

Nioka and her sons have to plant, tend and pick the crop. Once the bananas are harvested the family must grade, wash and pack them ready for export to the UK. Nioka's three eldest sons work on the farm while the youngest goes to school. If Nioka could not keep her business going she would have no hope for the future. Nioka is clear about the benefits of Fairtrade. Membership of a Fairtrade scheme allows her to 'get a better price and save more money'.

Before she became involved in Fairtrade through WINFA Nioka found life very hard. Now she is able to help with the education of her youngest son.

What your family could do

Introduction: Make a Fairtrade desert with your child/ren and, as you do so, look for opportunities to share Nioka's story. To find out stories about other Fairtrade growers visit the Fairtrade Foundation website at www.fairtrade.org.uk.

You will need: Fairtrade bananas
Fairtrade honey
Fairtrade chocolate
Selection of ice cream

Method
1 Peel your banana.
2 Cut the banana in half, lengthways.
3 Place two or three scoops of ice cream between the two halves of banana.
4 Grate a few chunks of Fairtrade chocolate and sprinkle over the top.
5 Drizzle with Fairtrade honey if desired.

PRAYER POINT

As they drizzle their honey, encourage your child/ren to try and use the honey to write words that mean 'fair' to them over the bananas and ice cream.

As you eat, share Nioka's story, which can be simplified as follows:
- Forty-three-year-old Nioka is a single mum with four sons between nine and twenty-six years of age. She is one of 605 small farmers who sell banana's to the Fairtrade market.
- Nioka's three eldest sons work on the farm while the youngest goes to school.
- Banana growing is tough. Nioka and her sons have to plant, tend and pick the crop, then grade, wash and pack them before they are ready to be exported to the UK.
- Bananas are the only way she can earn a decent living. As Nioka points out, 'They are what help me meet the needs of my family.'
- Membership of a Fairtrade scheme allows Nioka to 'get a better price and save more money'. Without her banana business, Nioka could not afford to send her youngest son to school.[74]

HELPFUL HINT

Try a Fairtrade fruit salad using Fairtrade fruit and Fairtrade juice. For more advanced Fairtrade recipes visit www.fairtrade.org.uk, go to 'Resources' and click on 'Recipes'.

Devotion 5

A FAIRTRADE CELEBRATION

AIMS: To consolidate what you've learnt about fairly traded products so far. To consider different ways of sharing your understanding of the benefits of buying fairly traded products.

What you ought to know

Eight hundred thousand people currently belong to Fairtrade cooperatives. The Fairtrade Foundation estimates that this impacts five million people from over 45 countries. The range of products currently stands at 800, but is growing all the time. As retailers see the increasing demand for Fairtrade they will begin to purchase more goods from cooperatives that will, in turn, be able to expand to include more farmers who are able to offer a wider range of produce. As farmers and cooperatives increase their supply and retailers begin to buy in bulk, the cost to the consumer will be able to become more competitive, but without affecting the prices paid to farmers who produce them. The more we choose Fairtrade, the more people will benefit. It would be nice to think that in the near future Fairtrade food would develop beyond a niche market to become the norm. Whether that happens is down to people like you passing on the benefits to others.

Tearfund's work on trade includes promoting the Fairtrade Mark and on fair trade through Tearcraft. In poorer countries, exploitation, rising costs and dwindling markets can sweep away the benefits of people's hard work. Few can find a fair price or a secure future in their local setting. Tearcraft provides an alternative market, paying workers in the poor communities a good price, and selling their crafts in the UK and Ireland. Tearfund also channels money into vital training for young people in Africa, Asia and Latin America, equipping them with skills that will help them to find jobs within their own communities. Through Small Enterprise Development (SED) and Income Generation (IG) projects, people can be enabled to own and manage their own businesses. These projects can bring a variety of long-term benefits, including management and administrative experience, income, jobs and technical skills. Tearfund believes that the issue of trade is important and essential to the lives of the world's poorest people.

What your family could do

Introduction: Consolidate what you've learnt about fairly traded products so far. Consider different ways of sharing your understanding of the benefits of buying fairly traded products with your:

- household
- wider family
- friends and neighbours.

You will need: paper, coloured pens or pencils, a selection of fairly traded goods

Design and draw a poster or invitation which shows the benefits of fairly traded goods. Use the understanding you have developed over previous devotions to inform your ideas about what you'd like to say and show. Things to think about might include:

- how the growers/producers are treated with Fairtrade and without Fairtrade.
- how people feel about Fairtrade
- the difference Fairtrade makes
- what you can buy fairly traded
- what you'd like to be able to buy which is fairly traded.

PRAYER POINT
Display your poster somewhere visible, for example in your dining room, by the breakfast table or on your fridge. Use it as a reminder to pray for people who produce your food and as an opportunity to actively share the benefits of Fairtrade with others.

You could use this as an opportunity to invite other family members or friends around to your home to taste Fairtrade food or to sample fairly traded products for themselves. You could use food you've baked or revisit your local supermarket and purchase a selection from there, for example cakes, biscuits, juices, teas or coffees. Have a selection of Tearcraft products available – or at least a catalogue. As a family, think about what a difference introducing Fairtrade options at school or church might make, both to the poor and to you.

HELPFUL HINT
Subscribe to the Fairtrade Foundation's newsletter 'Fair Comment' at www.fairtrade.org.uk/resources_newsletter.htm. Use it to remind you to pray for the Fairtrade Foundation on a regular basis.

Shopping for Food

Devotion 6

FROGS' LEGS?

AIMS: To think about the difference Tearcraft makes to people in poor communities. To develop an understanding of the difference we can make by buying products that have the Fairtrade Mark.

What you ought to know

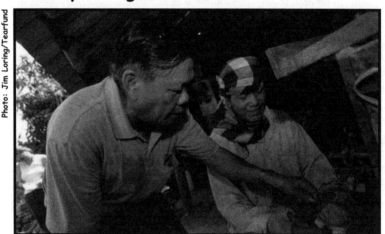

Oun Wongwiang is making a musical frog. If you stroke the frog's back with the stick you can hear him produce an amazing croaking sound.

As a young boy, Oun Wongwiang lived in a small hut at the back of his Thai home. No-one came to visit him, other than to leave food outside the door. His family shunned him because he had leprosy. They were scared that they would catch it if they came too near. When Oun was eighteen, his older brother learnt of the McKean Rehabilitation Centre, just outside Chiang Mai. There, Oun lived for six years.

Treatment for leprosy came too late to prevent his hands and feet being disfigured. But learning how to carve wood gave Oun ambitions for his own crafts business, Wongwiang Handicrafts. From humble beginnings, selling food to earn money to buy wood, Oun, aged fifty-five, now works with some 80 craftspeople across 15 villages in the Chiang Mai area. Some are based in workshops of up to 20 people, while others work from home, making items for Tearcraft.

'It's great to be able to help so many people have jobs,' he says. 'Sometimes I have not had enough work for them and I've had to send them away. That has been very hard.'

Oun feared job losses when the market for laquerware products started diminishing. But Tearfund small business consultant Rose Collins came up with new designs, and Wongwiang started making musical frogs and kitchen items. 'That has really helped,' he says.

What your family could do

Introduction: Play pass the parcel using Fairtrade food and an item from Tearcraft.

You will need: wrapping paper; cellotape; questions; music; Fairtrade items such as biscuits, chocolate, bananas, cereal bars, jam; a product/toy from Tearcraft (visit www.tearcraft.org for more information)

Make a Fairtrade food parcel. On alternative layers wrap one of the questions overleaf. In the other layers wrap a Fairtrade item such as biscuits, chocolate, bananas, cereal bars, jam and a product/toy from Tearcraft. Find some music and play pass the parcel. When the music stops, the person holding the parcel should tear off a layer and answer the question. Try to make sure that the adults get the questions and the children get the items. This would be a good game to play with other families.

Shopping for Food

Questions (answers are in bold)

1 The banana is the best selling food in a supermarket. On average, how many do you think one person eats in a year?[75]

    a) 30   b) 45   **c) 60**

2 If a bunch of bananas costs about £1, how much do you think the average grower will get?[76]

    a) 5p   **b) 7p**   c) 12p

3 Who drinks more coffee – mums or dads?[77]

    a) dads   b) mums

4 How much more might you expect to get for growing coffee if you are a Fairtrade farmer rather than a usual farmer?[78]

    a) 2.5 times   b) 5 times   c) 10 times

5 How much do you think people in the UK spend on Fairtrade in an average year?[79]

    a) £50 million   **b) £100 million**   c) £200 million

6 How many different Fairtrade items do you think there are?[80]

    a) 200   b) 400   **c) 800**

7 Which of these do you think are available to buy as Fairtrade?[81]

    a) Flowers   **b) Footballs**   **c) Fruit**
(yes, all of these are available)

Use this game to illustrate the benefits of Fairtrade and buying fairly traded products like Tearcraft.

PRAYER POINT
If you prefer, you could turn the game into a prayer parcel and include prayers about food and Fairtrade rather than questions.

Devotion 7

WORSHIPFUL LIFE

AIM: To provide an opportunity to reflect on what your children have learnt about Fairtrade and/or ethical clothing.

What you ought to know

Isaiah 58 is just one of many references to justice in the Bible. We find Israel questioning why their prayers don't seem to be getting answered, and God suggesting that it's all down to a little matter of integrity - they say one thing but do another. They fast, pray and worship with a passion, but their lives don't measure up. When we pray about justice do our lifestyle choices also echo our demands? Do the clothes we wear, or the snacks we consume, contribute to or combat the injustice we pray about? Which screams loudest to God, our words or our actions?

Presumably, rather than songs, what God really wants is a worship filled lifestyle full of activity that benefits others. A life that doesn't just sing about our desire to 'loose the chains of injustice' (Is. 58:6-7), but actually demonstrates it. God wants a life emptied, given over and completely spent for the sake of someone other than ourselves (Is. 58:10-12). It's hard to dispute that God's into justice, or that he requires us to be too (Mich. 6:8), so perhaps the question for our families ought to be not 'whether?', but 'how?'

If you really want to impact people thousands of miles away living in poorer countries, there is no easier way than to buy the food or crafts that they produce - but for a fair price! Buying goods that are fairly traded is just one way you can impact global trade on a personal level. Your simple shopping habits could help to improve people's homes, support their education and healthcare, build roads, and help them to invest more in their businesses. When you shop, look out for the Fairtrade Mark. When you next think about buying a gift for someone, check out Tearcraft.

What your family could do

Introduction: Use *Photograph 9* to reflect upon how we should spend money. Discuss and pray about issues surrounding shopping, by considering:
- what we need to remember
- what is incredible
- what is a challenge
- what is encouraging.

You will need: *Photograph 9* (Poster Pack/CD-ROM)

Use the photograph as a stimulus to reflect upon what you have learnt about fairly traded goods and ethical clothing. Use your reflection to form the basis of your prayers, for example:

Remember – the people behind the products we buy; the conditions they work in and the long hours they work.

Incredible – that the workers get paid so little in comparison with how much we pay. Thank God for the Fairtrade Foundation and the Ethical Trade Initiative, that are both working to ensure workers are paid fairly.

Challenge – ask God to challenge you to change your spending habits to benefit other people.

Encouraging – that how we choose to use our money has a direct effect on people all over the world. We can make a difference.

> **PRAYER POINT**
> Please refer to the above as an example. God speaks to us all differently. He may have said specific things to you as a family. Use the above as a structure for focus and prayer. It's easy to remember, just think R.I.C.E!

6 Education

What follows is a series of devotions designed to enable your family to connect with the issues of school, education and God's heart for the poor. Work through in order or choose as many or as few as seems appropriate to your context. Most of us, and children in particular, learn best by doing, so whilst some are reflective, the majority of these activities are practical. It is important that all family members are involved, not just the children, as actions that develop thinking and change habits are generally ones which we learn together and from one another.

Your devotions on education will help you to:

1 understand the role of parents and children within a family
2 understand the effect people have on our lives
3 understand what a school in another part of the world is like
4 understand why children miss out on school
5 consider how a lack of education can impact girls
6 reflect on how important education is in breaking the cycle of poverty
7 identify the difference education can make.

Your way in

Everyday situations that your child/ren might face, or natural conversations that you might have as a family, will provide some of the best ways in to exploring the issue of education and the poor. Look out for things your child/ren say and do as they begin to widen their perspective of their whole wide world and use these as a stimulus or way in to the subject in question.

Education

WHAT YOUR CHILD/REN MIGHT...

DO	SAY
Fail to do their homework	'Do I have to go to school?'
Look forward to weekends and holiday	'I hate school.'
	'But school's boring.'
Complain about school	'Why does everyone have to go to school?'
Not understand why school is so important	'Does everyone have to go to school?'
Talk about what they want to be when they get 'bigger'	'Why do I have to go to school?'
Hate school	'Why can't some children go to school?'
Love school	
Make friends	'Did you go to school?'
Value their teachers	'Did you like school?'
Bring home work they've done at school	'When I grow up I want to be a...'

Devotion 1

HOUSE RULES

AIM: To understand the role of parents and children within a family.

What you ought to know

What have you learnt today, during the past week or month? It might be learning how to use the latest piece of technology or how to fill out a form – we are learning all the time. We learn in different ways. Some people learn visually, by taking information from what they see. Other people are auditory learners – they learn by listening. Some people are kinaesthetic learners – they learn by doing. Whatever our learning style, we all deserve the right to learn, to develop our knowledge and understanding and to acquire new skills.

Jesus spent a great deal of time teaching and preaching. When he did, he often used people's own experience as a starting point (Mt. 9:16–17). He told many stories to communicate his message, but also to make people think (Mt. 13:34). He also used everyday objects to make tangible connections between people's lives and his teaching (Mt. 6:26–29). Finally, rather than coming at people with all the answers he would ask questions in order to involve them in the process of meeting their needs (Mt. 6:25–28). The Bible is packed full of good advice on how to make better choices about life. As powerful as God's word is, if we don't put what it teaches us into action, then words is all it really is. The thing that distinguished Jesus' teaching from most of that which preceded it was that his works and his wonders backed up his words. He lived out what he taught. We all need to learn from Jesus' example on how to love God and love others.

Consider how your children learn from you. What do they learn from your actions? What do they learn from what you say? The

Education

relationship between parents and children is important. Young children learn most from what their parent/s or carer/s do and say. As children get older, and the circle of people they know grows wider, they look to other adults as well. But when your child/ren are young you have the most influence.

What your family could do

Introduction: Read together what Paul said to the people of Ephesus in Ephesians 6:1-4.

You will need: a children's Bible: try the *International Children's Bible*, published by Authentic Media

Split the verses into two parts.

A child's responsibility
Part 1: verses 1-3

> Children obey your parents the way the Lord wants you to. This is the right thing to do. The command says, 'Honour your mother and father.' This is the first command that has a promise with it. The promise is: 'Then everything will be well with you, and you will have a long life on the earth.' [82]

Read and then consider what this means to you as a family. When is it right to obey? Parents, what should you be asking your child/ren? Explain to your child/ren why you ask them to do certain things.

The parents' responsibility
Part 2: verse 4

> Fathers [and mothers], do not make your children angry, but raise them with the training and teaching of the Lord. [83]

Read and then consider what this means to you as a family. It is a partnership; parents and children need to work together. You are in the unique position as a parent – you can share and show what it really means to be a friend of Jesus.

Write a set of positive family rules – considering how you should treat each other. As a family, think about the different areas the Ten Commandments cover (Ex.20), i.e. relationship with God, others and each other. Make sure your family rules value God, others and yourself. Make sure the rules are what you 'can' do, not what you 'can't', for example 'speak politely and respect each other' rather than 'don't be rude or shout'.

HELPFUL HINT

The responsibilities of the poor
The rules you write will be determined in part by the different roles you feel each member of your family has to play each day. You may find it a helpful exercise to think through how your rules might be different if you lived in a poor family, for example:

- How would the need to walk to collect water twice a day impact what you wrote?
- What about the impact of climate change on your responsibilities, or lack of food? How would these change/shape your rules?

PRAYER POINT

Over the next few days pray about each rule in turn. Discuss what each rule means to your family in practical terms.

Education

Devotion 2

WHY LEARN?

AIMS: To develop an understanding of the effect people have on our lives. To identify key areas of learning.

What you ought to know

Through school, children learn and develop skills in literacy and numeracy. So why is education so vital for children living in a poor country? What difference will it make? It's simple: if children can't read and write, or do simple maths, they are more likely to be exploited and will find it difficult to make wise choices or find a good job. Educated people are much more likely to know their rights. Even though jobs may be hard to come by in poor communities, if children are able to go to school they will stand a better chance of getting any that may exist. Education can be the difference between life and death. Even if, as we have seen in Chapter 4, wages are low, if an individual is able to work there is some hope of them being able to earn money to live on, which should lead to a healthier life. Educated people are more aware of health issues. Educated communities can work and plan together and take initiatives and make decisions that will positively impact their future.

Jurain is one the most violent districts in Dhaka, Bangladesh. Young girls are at risk from robbery, drugs, rape and murder. Tearfund's partner Heed Bangladesh runs a Women's and Children's Education Programme (WCEP), where teenage girls are paid a small wage to teach younger children free of charge. Younger girls improve their chances of getting to school, whilst older girls earn the money they need to continue their education. With education and knowledge, the future of girls who are part of WCEP, holds so many more possibilities. These are some of the WCEP girls:

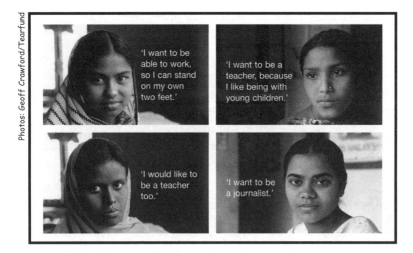

At their school in Bangladesh, Noyontara (top left), Lipi (top right), Shilpi (bottom left) and Suchander all dream about their future.

What your family could do

Introduction: Encourage your children to dream about their future. Consider whether achieving your ambition is in any way influenced by the country you happened to be born in.

You will need: magazines, catalogues, large sheets of paper, scissors, glue, *Photograph 10* (Poster Pack/CD-ROM).

Collect lots of magazines and catalogues. Use the pictures to make a collage of the people and places that affect our learning. As you are doing this activity, discuss why learning is so important and what the child/ren's aspirations are – what they want to do when they are older. How are they going to achieve their aims? Share with your child/ren the skills you want to develop. Help them understand that learning is continual; it is not just something that children do.

- How do you think your children's dreams about the future differ from or match those of children living in poor communities?
- Share *Photograph 10* and read each speech bubble.

- Discuss what might get in the way of these children realizing their dreams.

It is important to note that whatever dreams children might have in poor countries, education alone will not be sufficient to provide people with a quick route out of poverty. As well as some of the issues covered within this book, factors such as disease, conflict and how the world's economy is structured in favour of the rich at the expense of the poor all need to be tackled if we're ever to overcome poverty once and for all.

> **PRAYER POINT**
> Pray for each member of your family in turn. Thank God for them. Thank God they do have dreams. Ask God to help them to take the appropriate steps to fulfil their dreams. Pray for children from other countries like Suchander, Lipi, Shilpi and Noyontara, that they will have the opportunities to learn and develop so that their dreams become a reality.

Devotion 3

WHAT A DAY!

AIM: To develop an understanding of what a school in another part of the world is like.

What you ought to know

Furahini is seven years old and attends Uhambingeto Primary School in Tanzania, a school supported by Tearfund partner The Diocese of Ruaha. There are an incredible 676 children at the school sharing six classrooms and just eight teachers. Furahini is in Standard Two, the second year of primary school. Children used to start school at eight years old, but since Tanzania received debt relief, children have been able to start school from the age of six.

Before Furahini leaves for school at 7 a.m. she will eat her breakfast – a cup of tea and a light snack – and sweep the yard clean for her mother. After walking her four-year-old brother Shadrach (Shady for short) to kindergarten, Furahini usually walks the rest of the way alone. Some of the children in her school walk as far as ten miles, from the other side of the mountains that surround her village. Furahini's walk is much less, but still takes her down the only main road in and out of the village.

The day begins in the yard with games followed by assembly. In class, Furahini learns simple mathematics: 1 + 1 = 2, 2 + 2 = 4, 4 + 4 = 8, and so on. The children sing the days of the week in English. There's no sign of any books, pencils or the kind of resources we might expect to see in UK schools. At break time there's more time to play and sing together. After school it's Furahini's job to collect and prepare food for the evening meal, leaving just enough time to sweep, do a few other general

Education

household chores and, of course, homework. After dinner at 6 p.m. there's just time to get ready for bed before it gets dark at 7 p.m.

What your family could do

Introduction: Watch *Video 2: My Whole Day* together. As you watch, encourage your child/ren to think about what they would be doing at school that is similar to/different from Furahini.

You will need: *Printable 10: Timetable, Video 2: My Whole Day* (CD-ROM)

The video includes the following elements representing a day in the life of a Tanzanian primary school child:

- jobs before school
- getting to school
- assembly
- in class
- in the playground
- jobs after school
- doing homework.

After you have watched the video ask your child/ren to pick a time of day and to draw or write something from their own day in one box and something from Furahini's day in the other. The printable 'timetable' on the CD-ROM might help your child/ren's thinking.

	Before school	During school	After school
Me			
Furahini			

As well as her education, Furahini also enjoys all the jobs she has to do after school, including helping to get the dinner ready.

Use the table to discuss the differences and similarities between your child/ren's day at school and Furahini's, for example how they get to school, who they go with, what they have to take, resources and facilities they have whilst at school.

PRAYER POINT
Before and after school, pray for children like Furahini.

Devotion 4

THE VALUE OF EDUCATION

AIM: To understand why children miss out on school.

What you ought to know

For millions of children around the world, education is not even a possibility. Over 100 million children miss out on an education worldwide; more than half of them are girls.[84] Children miss school for a number of different reasons:

- Many places lack either schools or qualified teachers.
- Sometimes there are teachers but the government cannot afford to pay them so they can't teach.
- If children have special needs or disabilities, schools often struggle to support them.
- Some children have to work instead of going to school to help their families survive.
- Education isn't free in all countries, and some parents can't afford the fees.
- Some children have no families to support them; they may be orphaned or may have run away – sleeping on the streets even basic survival is a struggle.

A lack of local schooling or insufficient teachers presents a huge barrier to a child's ability to access education. However, the resourcefulness of children and their unrelenting desire to receive education at any cost is staggering. Primary school-aged children will travel as far as 10 miles in order to get to school, often through thick grasses, on dangerous roads and even over mountains. Some secondary school girls in Tanzania are travelling an incredible 20 miles to school, a journey that may take them several days to complete. The sad thing is that despite their efforts, without adequate clothing, shoes, stationery, books and school or examination fees, many of them will be turned away at the gate.

What your family could do

Introduction: Thank God that we can access education. Pray for children that live in countries where governments don't provide education for all children.

You will need: *Photograph 11* (Poster Pack/CD-ROM)

Allow your child/ren to collect as much information as they can from the photograph itself. Ask your child/ren to describe what they can see. Use your discussion to form the basis of your prayers, considering:

- what we need to remember
- what is incredible
- what is a challenge
- what is encouraging.

For example:

Remember – around 125 million children miss out on an education for several reasons. Pray that through the work of key organizations this will start to change.

Incredible – education gives choices and can be the difference between life and death.

Challenge – to be thankful for the education that we receive and to make the most of it.

Encouraging – if children do go to school, they have a better chance of getting a job that pays enough money to live on, leading to a healthier life.

> **PRAYER POINT**
> Please refer to the above as an example. God speaks to us all differently. He may have said specific things to you as a family. Use the above as a structure for focus and prayer. It's easy to remember, just think R.I.C.E!

Education

Devotion 5

CHILDREN AT RISK

AIM: To understand how the lack of a chance of an education can have a long-term impact on girls in particular. To consider what our response should be to people who are prevented from going to school because of a lack of money.

What you ought to know

Halima Msiyura is fourteen years old and a pupil at Uhambingeto Primary School in Tanzania, a project supported by Tearfund partner the Diocese of Ruaha. Halima is in Standard Seven sitting her internal (MOC) exams in maths and science. They are designed to expose any gaps in her learning and to strengthen up any weaknesses that she may have which would prevent her from qualifying to go to secondary school. If Halima fails her final exam she has two choices:

- to go to the city to earn money working as a house girl
- to stay in her village.

Even if Halima passes, she may not get the chance to go to secondary school. Primary education in Tanzania is now free. Debt relief has enabled the government to abolish primary school fees, leading to a 66 per cent increase in attendance.[85] Secondary education costs money. Her parents need to find the money to pay her fees: 100,000 Tanzanian shillings per term (approx. £49), or 200,000 Tanzanian shillings per term (approx. £98) if she boards.

If her family can't find the fees, Halima will have to consider taking a job as a house girl. Open to abuse, many house girls return to their village suffering from an unwanted pregnancy or HIV and AIDS. Some of the girls in a nearby village have taken the option to become house girls. Many even leave the same night they sit their exams, before they get their results, because they know their families can't afford their education. Either trucks from the city come to pick them up (offering 'large' sums of money to families) or the girls embark on a seven-hour journey by bus or a journey taking many days by foot.

What your family could do

Introduction: Think as a family about all the things you need in order to go to school, from pencils to books to uniforms. Consider what you could do to help others to go to school.

You will need: *Photograph 12* (Poster Pack/CD-ROM), drawing materials

Explain Halima's story using *Photograph 12* – ensure you keep the content appropriate to the age of your child/ren. For example:

- Halima Msiyura is fourteen years old and a pupil at Uhambingeto Primary School in Tanzania.
- She is sitting an exam in Maths and Science.
- If Halima fails she will have to chose whether to leave her family to go to the city to earn money working as a house girl (a kind of servant) or stay in her village.
- Even if Halima passes, she may not get the chance to go to secondary school if her parents can't find the money to pay her fees: approx. £49 per term.
- What would you spend this much money on?

Our government funds education in the UK. Discuss how each member of your family would feel if a child had to leave because you couldn't afford the fees for them to go to school.

Consider how you as a family could help other families who are struggling to pay school fees. Draw pictures of everything you need for school from pens and pencils to textbooks and school uniforms.

Tearfund partners support families in poor communities by subsidizing school fees, running loan schemes to allow families to earn money by growing crops, and even building schools. Tearfund's Children at Risk programme provides an ideal opportunity to support children in desperate need of schooling all over the world. Join and your support will transform young lives. You will receive a welcome pack with: a mini CD-ROM, poster, prayer card, campaign card and the first of your regular six-monthly updates. Each update voices the concerns and dreams of groups of children around the world, in their own words. They will challenge and inspire you and your family.

PRAYER POINT

As a family, pray through your response to the needs you have learned about. You could give regularly through Tearfund's Children at Risk scheme or perhaps the next time you buy a uniform or school related equipment you could put aside the equivalent amount of money and send it to Tearfund to allow them to support children through their schooling.

Devotion 6

BUILDING A BETTER FUTURE

AIM: To reflect on how it's important to find ways to break the poverty cycle through education.

What you ought to know

Without education, the threat of abuse, unwanted pregnancies and catching diseases such as HIV and AIDS greatly increases, particularly for girls. In sub-Saharan Africa 40 per cent of girls are not educated.[86] To see any improvement in the quality of life thus far, and for any hope of a better future, it is key that girls and women are educated. Girls are often more likely to miss out on schooling because:

- they are kept at home to help with household tasks
- in some places families believe that they don't need to be educated
- some families who struggle to pay school fees tend to send the boys
- girls may not have the proper sanitary protection to enable them to attend school regularly and confidently.

Girl or boy, man or woman, without education it can be almost impossible to break out of a desperate cycle of poverty.

Education

If you have had no education…

…you and your family are unable to earn enough money.

Without money…

…you are unable to have access to adequate food, healthcare or education.

If you have had no education…

…you and your family are unable to earn enough money.

And so on…

The poverty cycle can affect a whole country. If a population is in poverty, little money can be raised in taxes. This means that the government is poor and is unable to invest in key services such as education. Poverty cycles need to be broken. Along with the other issues we've covered in this book, education is just one point at which we can begin to break into the effects of poverty.

What your family could do

Introduction: Play a game to help your family understand the role of education in tackling poverty.

You will need: *Printable 11: Body parts game* (CD-ROM) – one set of body parts each and the spinner, card (from a used cereal box if it goes through your printer, or corrugated if you chose to print out the body parts and stick them to card to strengthen them), a pencil to use with your spinner

Cut out the body parts and place them in a pile.

Photo: Phil Bowyer

Education

The aim of this game is to collect the different parts of a person – head, body, two legs and two arms – and to make a person. In turn, each person spins the spinner.

To start you need to pick up the body by spinning the spinner and landing on EDUCATION. The arms and the legs can then be collected in any order. Spin the spinner and land on a:

- good JOB to pick up a **right leg**
- money for FOOD to pick up a **right arm**
- money for a HOUSE to pick up a **left arm**
- money for MEDICINE to pick up a **left leg**.

You need to land on LIFE to pick up a head in order to finish.

Through this game you should be able to explain appropriately the difference that having an education makes to peoples lives. From having an education, you have a better chance of getting a good job, which gives you money for food and a house, access to healthcare, and the ability to make choices. Each person should end up with a 'person' who is strong because they started with an education and who is able to make better choices that will positively impact their future and the future of generations to come.

PRAYER POINT
After the game use each body part and pray for what it represents, i.e. medicine, housing, food, etc.

The Whole Wide World **145**

Education

Devotion 7

WHAT A DIFFERENCE A DAY MAKES

Aim: To understand the difference education can make.

What you ought to know

Hannah, aged ten, Kume, aged thirteen, and Kume's brother Gataneh, who's also ten, all live in a remote village in Ethiopia (see *Photograph 11*). They live in a valley so isolated that it has no running water, no electricity, no roads and, until recently, no school. Now Hannah, Kume and Gataneh all receive informal education from Meserete Kristos Church, a Tearfund partner in Meta Robi, Ethiopia. With the help they are receiving, their future prospects have changed considerably.

Before starting school, Kume had to help her mother in every household activity, particularly fetching the water, collecting firewood, and helping out with farming tasks. She says: 'I hate what I had to do, the work that I was doing before I went to school. It was a very boring life.'

Now Kume is top of her class and wants to be a doctor. Education is a remarkable gift for Kume. Her future, it seems, has only just begun. She says: 'How do you think? How does anyone think, before you have a chance of an education? How can you think about your future? I didn't have anything to think about, I didn't have any idea.'

In other parts of Ethiopia some children are still unable to access education. Misre can't afford to go to school. Misre says: 'I really enjoyed learning, when my family first sent me to school. But later on they asked me to stop because I had to work for money instead. I am very sad because of that. I am still hoping to have an education. I hope to become a doctor.'

Misre is one of 125 million children world wide who miss out on education every day.

What your family could do

Introduction: Join Hannah on her way to school to discover how similar/different her journey to school is from yours.

You will need: counters (e.g. different types of coin), a die or spinner, Board game: *School Run* (Poster Pack).

Use the board game 'School Run' from the Poster Pack to play a game about school. Players can choose whether to be Hannah from Ethiopia or Tom from the UK. Make sure at least one player chooses the alternative route to school.

During the game, ensure you take opportunities to share Hannah and Misre's story, which can be summarized as follows:

- Hannah is ten years old.
- In her village in Ethiopia they have no
  - running water
  - electricity
  - roads (if you want to go anywhere you have to go by donkey or walk for miles and miles and miles).
- But there are
  - chickens
  - families
  - and now there's a school!
- Misre has been stopped from going to school.
- The family needs money so send Misre to work instead of going to school.
- Misre is very sad but still dreams of becoming a doctor.

PRAYER POINT
After the game, reflect on what you have learnt, return to the board and pray for children who find accessing education difficult by considering:

- what we need to remember
- what is incredible
- what is a challenge
- what is encouraging.

Just remember R.I.C.E.

Use your reflection to form the basis of your prayers, for example:

Remember – that all children can't go to school. Think about Misre's story in particular.

Incredible – that children in other countries seem to be prepared to go to any lengths in order to get an education, whilst in the UK some of us seem to do anything we can to get out of going to school.

Challenge – ask God to challenge you to appreciate the education you do have.

Encouraging – that with your help Tearfund partners can help even more children to go to school.

Conclusion

The kingdom of heaven is like a mustard seed, which a man took and planted in his field. (Mt. 13:31)

Small beginnings

You may have finished the book, but for the sake of the poor it's imperative that you and your family continue to think about creative ways to use the resources and opportunities you have to become people of long-term influence. At this point you will either feel completely inspired to take grand decisions about your life or rather small in comparison to the kind of world we've spent the last six chapters describing. It is important that you hold on to the fact that you have seen that through small changes to your simple, everyday lifestyle choices it is possible to make a big difference to personal, national and global situations.

> *Though it is the smallest of all your seeds, yet when it grows, it is the largest of garden plants and becomes a tree, so that the birds of the air come and perch in its branches.' (Mt. 13:32)*

We can all have an influence in our world, no matter how small we might feel – the important thing is that we make a start and get more involved. The parable of the mustard seed is a great biblical example of how Jesus encourages us to exercise our faith and to look for ways to grow the potential we all have to influence the kinds of situations that exist in his world. Think for a minute about the qualities of that seed, which Jesus uses to describe how he would have his kingdom come.

At the bottom of our garden there's an apple tree in a pot. It hasn't always been an apple tree; it used to be a seed. Our neighbour gave it to us just after our child Zach was born.

Zach's now five and the tree is almost twice as big as him. It used to be hard to explain to Zach that one day that tiny little twig was going to provide him with as much fruit as he could eat – which would be a lot, as he loves fruit. It must have been a hard concept for him to accept, as, to him, apples were extremely heavy and the twig felt super bendy. It's now easier for him to believe that one day it will bear fruit, but he still hasn't seen it. One day he will. One day the tree will bear fruit; it's just that it's still not quite strong enough to cope with the weight of a crop. But ready or not, so far everything the sapling has done has been leading up to the day when it will bear fruit that will be good enough to eat.

It's amazing to think that everything Zach's tree needs to produce fruit was already contained within that tiny seed that our neighbour planted on our behalf all those years ago. All it needed was the right mixture of circumstances and a bit of effort on our part to get things moving in the right direction. One thing we've learnt as a family, as we've watched, watered and occasionally weeded this young tree, is that although there may be no short cut from seed to fruit, what keeps us going is the hope that one day we will taste the fruits of our labour. Though we may not be sure when exactly that will be, in faith we keep going, taking as many simple steps as we can in order to ensure that we have done all we can in order to add something beneficial to our world.

Each of us, each family, contains everything God needs to produce something of worth for the sake of our world. Something fruitful that could be of great benefit to the poor. We just need to ensure we are all doing what we can, where we are and whenever we can. Actions that may start small and go unnoticed all have the potential to grow into something visibly significant – where would the birds in Matthew 13 have found any refuge without the initial efforts of that tiny mustard seed? Whatever we choose to plant today, or tomorrow, we simply don't know the impact it will have on the future. In the beginning, Jesus' early ministry relied on him going to small numbers of people to make small differences to their lives, but as his influence on their lives grew so did his impact (Mt. 4:23, cf. 15:29-31).

So start small

In order to grow something of substance, whether a one-off action or a lifestyle change, we need to be careful not to dismiss small beginnings (see Zech. 4:10), but to use whatever connections we have to the issues in order to make the most of every opportunity that may come our way (see Col. 4:5; Eph. 5:15-17). We've thought a lot about the ways in which we're connected to others through the similarity of the things we do in our lives. Just because we're different in the resources we have at our disposal, it does not make us any less connected to the lives of the poor. You have to start somewhere. Even if at this moment you're feeling world domination is beyond you, it's important that you remember to start where you are with what you know. Rather than overlook small beginnings as we search to make a big splash, we need to begin to look closer to home in order to begin to make a real difference. Try this simple exercise. Draw a circle with four zones:

- In the centre write your own name or the name of your family.
- In Zone A write the daily activities in which you invest your time – e.g. eating, shopping, watching TV, playing sport.
- In Zone B write the people groups these activities bring you into contact with, either locally, nationally or globally.
- In Zone C write those issues which either affect them or concern you, or simply things which you are interested or involved in some way – e.g. the environment, reading, fishing.

Think big

Already you should be beginning to build a picture of just how connected you are to global situations by your everyday actions.

We all need to use the regular choices God gives us to bring about whatever changes we can. You could give your time and money, but even if you feel you have little of either, hopefully this book has helped you to see how simple involvement is, provided you are prepared to:

Stop – and learn more about the situations or issues that impact your 'neighbours' locally, nationally and globally.

Look – for opportunities to begin to make changes to your own life in order to impact theirs.

Listen – and pray to God about how you can make a difference to their lives.

Should you feel you want to take matters further, you might want to encourage your family to think about ways of becoming advocates for the poor, people who speak out and lobby decision makers to bring about positive change for the sake of others. Think about the kind of things you might want to ask people who already have influence in our world. It's easier than you might think. All you need to do is ensure you know the facts about your concern (Tearfund's website and the links at the end of this book will help you here) and are clear about a few simple points that you would want to ask or request of them.

> **HELPFUL HINT**
> It's important to remember that any campaigns that you feel you'd like to get involved in will tend to have more impact when large numbers of people do the same action. Keep up to date with all the latest action on the issues we've covered – start by visiting www.tearfund.org/campaigning. Tearfund's Whose Earth? Campaign is particularly important if you're interested in taking action on poverty and the environment, including climate change. Of course, campaigns that seem youth or adult focused will require you to be creative in order to ensure they are accessible to your family.

Dig deep

Being a person of influence is about having the wisdom to choose to do something that seems worthwhile and has the potential to grow – prayer is the best way to discover what that might be! Never stop praying about ways you can influence situations for the better. Make a commitment to see it through until you see the fruit. As a family or group you may feel the need to make some form of commitment to what you've experienced together throughout this book. Take some strips of paper, a plant pot, compost and an apple seed. Encourage everyone to write down on their piece of paper one thing that they'll commit to do in the next hours, weeks, months and years. Place the paper at the base of the pot, cover with compost and plant the seed. Use the growing seed as a reminder of your commitment. Ask God to help keep you on track and see how your influence on God's whole wide world grows when you take matters into your own hands!

> *And I [we] pray that you, being rooted and established in love, may have power, together with all the saints, to grasp how wide and long and high and deep is the love of Christ, and to know this love that surpasses knowledge – that you may be filled to the measure of all the fullness of God. (Eph. 3:17-19)*

Going Deeper

Further information

Tearfund

Tearfund is an evangelical Christian relief and development agency working through local partners to bring help and hope to communities in need around the world. The purpose of Tearfund is to serve Jesus Christ by enabling those who share evangelical Christian beliefs to bring good news to the poor.

'Global Action' is Tearfund's free quarterly campaigning magazine, with regular email updates. To keep up to date with campaigns and to sign up to receive globalaction: Visit: www.tearfund.org/globalaction.
To find out more about Tearfund:
Visit: www.tearfund.org
Email: enquiry@tearfund.org
Phone: 0845 355 8355 (ROI: +44 845 355 8355)
Write to: Tearfund, 100 Church Road, Teddington, Middlesex TW11 8QE, England.

Water and sanitation

To find out more about Tearfund's campaigns:
Visit: www.tearfund.org/campaigning
Email: enquiry@tearfund.org

WaterAid is the UK's only major charity dedicated to the provision of safe domestic water, sanitation and hygiene promotion to the world's poorest people. To find out more:

Visit: www.wateraid.org
Phone: 020 7793 4500
Write to: Prince Consort House, 27-29 Albert Embankment, London SE1 7UB

Going Deeper

Weather and energy

To find out more about Tearfund's campaigns:

Visit: www.tearfund.org/campaigning
Email: enquiry@tearfund.org

Whose Earth? is a Tearfund campaign that looks at the links between poverty and the environment. For more information and to take action on climate change or water and sanitation:

Visit: www.tearfund.org/whoseearth
Phone: 0845 355 8355

Energy Efficient Advice Centre offers advice on reducing energy wastage and can tell you about grants and offers available. To find out more:

Phone: 0800 512 012

Energy Saving Trust is one of the UK's leading organizations tasked with sustainable energy solutions in homes and on the road. To find out more:

Visit: www.est.org.uk
Phone: 020 7222 0101
Write to: 21 Dartmouth Street, London SW1H 9BP

Friends of the Earth inspires solutions to environmental problems to make life better for people. To find out more:

Visit: www.foe.org.uk
Phone: 0808 800 1111
Write to: 26–28 Underwood Street, London N1 7JQ

'Green' electricity means electricity produced from sources that do not cause harmful impacts upon the environment. Of course, every type of electricity generation will have some impact, but some sources are much greener than others. The cleanest energy sources are those that utilize the natural energy flows of the earth. These are usually known as 'renewable' energy sources, because they will never run out. To find out more:

Visit: www.greenelectricity.org

Recycle-More is a one-stop recycling information centre. You will find help and advice on all aspects of recycling at home, at school and in the workplace. To find out more:

Visit: www.recycle-more.co.uk

Sustrans is a charity that works on practical projects to encourage people to walk, cycle and use public transport. To find out more:

Visit: www.sustrans.org.uk
Phone: 0117 926 8893
Write to: National Cycle Network Centre, 2 Cathedral Square, College Green, Bristol BS1 5DD

Transport 2000 is the independent national body concerned with sustainable transport. It looks for answers to transport problems and aims to reduce the environmental and social impact of transport by encouraging less use of cars and more use of public transport, walking and cycling. To find out more:

Visit: www.transport2000.org.uk
Phone: 020 7613 0743
Write to: The Impact Centre, 12-18 Hoxton Street, London N1 6NG

Food

To find out more about Tearfund's campaigns:

Visit: www.tearfund.org/campaigning
Email: enquiry@tearfund.org

Disaster Emergency Committee, an umbrella organization uniting 13 of the UK's major aid agencies, launches and co-ordinates the UK's National Appeal in response to major disasters overseas. Its members are: ActionAid, British Red Cross, CAFOD, CARE International UK, Christian Aid, Concern, Help the Aged, Islamic Relief, Merlin, Oxfam, Save the Children, Tearfund and World Vision. To find out more:

Visit: www.dec.org.uk
Phone: 020 7387 0200
Write to: 15 Warren Mews, London W1T 6AZ

FareShare supplies 12,000 meals a day to homeless and vulnerable people using surplus food provided by supermarkets. There are eight FareShare schemes operating in partnership with local charities across the UK, working in partnership with over 150 companies and 250 local charities.

Visit: www.fareshare.org.uk
Phone: 020 7394 2468
Write to: FareShare, Unit H04, Tower Bridge Business Complex, 100 Clements Road, Bermondsey, London SE16 4DG
Email: enquiries@fareshare.org.uk

Shopping for clothes and food

Tearcraft is Tearfund's fair trade business. Tearcraft exists to benefit skilled artisans from some of the world's poorest communities, helping them to create and market products of the highest standard and ensure that a fair price is paid for their work. For a catalogue:

Visit: www.tearcraft.org
Phone: 0870 240 4896

Lift the Label is Tearfund's ethical lifestyle campaign for students and young people. For more information and resources on ethical food, fashion and finance:

Visit: www.tearfund.org/liftthelabel
Phone: 0845 355 8355

Clean Clothes Campaign has four areas of activity – raising public awareness, solidarity work, pressuring companies and developing legal initiatives. In the UK it operates through Labour behind the Label. To find out more information:

Email: info@cleanclothes.org
Visit: www.cleanclothes.org
Phone: 00 3120 412 2785
Write to: PO Box 115841001, GN Amsterdam, Netherlands

Equal Exchange is a fair trade company supplying a range of fair trade food and drink. For more information:

Phone: 0131 554 5912
Write to: Equal Exchange Trading Ltd, 10a Queensferry Street, Edinburgh EH2 4PG

Fairtrade Foundation exists to ensure a better deal for marginalized and disadvantaged producers in poor countries. The Foundation awards a consumer label, the Fairtrade Mark, to products that meet internationally recognized standards of fair trade. For more information on products, suppliers, resources and how to get more involved:

Visit: www.fairtrade.org.uk
Email: mail@fairtrade.org.uk
Phone: 020 7405 5942 (general), 020 7242 9632 (resources)
Write to: Fairtrade Foundation, Room 204, 16 Baldwin's Gardens, London EC1N 7RJ

Labour behind the Label is a UK network of organizations supporting garment workers' efforts to defend their rights and improve their wages and conditions. It includes major overseas aid organizations, major UK textile unions, home working organizations and small solidarity groups. To find out more information:

Visit: www.labourbehindthelabel.org
Email: lbl@gn.apc.org
Phone: 01603 666160
Write to: 38 Exchange Street, Norwich NR2 1AX

Going Deeper

People Tree works with 70 Fairtrade groups in 20 countries, giving design and technical assistance to marginalized producers struggling to sell their products. People Tree pays a fair price, gives advance credit when needed, and commits to ordering regularly. To find out more:

Visit: www.ptree.co.uk

Trade Justice Movement links organizations concerned about the negative impact of trade on the world's poorest people. Tearfund is a member. They work together to put pressure on the UK government to take the lead in international negotiations to change the rules for better. For more information:

Visit: www.tradejusticemovement.org.uk

Traidcraft has the UK's widest range of fair trade products. For a catalogue or to buy selected items online:

Visit: www.traidcraftshop.co.uk
Email: help@traidcraft.co.uk
Phone: 0870 443 1018
Write to: Traidcraft plc, Kingsway, Gateshead, Tyne and Wear NE11 0NE

Education

To find out more about Tearfund's campaigns:

Visit: www.tearfund.org
Email: enquiry@tearfund.org

Jubilee Debt Campaign (JDC) is the UK's campaigning successor to Jubilee 2000 and Drop the Debt – a coalition of regional groups and national organizations whose focus is on changing UK government policy on debt and influencing the policies of the World Bank and International Monetary Fund. Tearfund is a member. To find out more:

Visit: www.jubileedebtcampaign.org.uk
Email: info@jubileedebtcampaign.org.uk

Phone: 020 7324 4722

Write to: The Grayston Centre, 28 Charles Square, London N1 6HT

Parentscentre provides information and support for parents on how to help with your child's learning, including advice on choosing a school and finding childcare. To find out more:

Visit: www.parentscentre.gov.uk

Glossary

aid	financial or material assistance, for example that provided by a government or international organization, especially in times of crisis.
AIDS	stands for Acquired Immune Deficiency Syndrome. AIDS describes the collection of symptoms and infections, for example chest infections, digestive disorders, cancer and brain disease, which are associated with acquired deficiency of the immune system. (See also details about HIV.)
atmosphere	a gravitational field strong enough to prevent the mixture of gases surrounding the earth from escaping. The earth's atmosphere is composed of: nitrogen (78 per cent) and oxygen (21 per cent). The remaining 1 per cent is argon (0.9 per cent), carbon dioxide (0.03 per cent), varying amounts of water vapour and trace amounts of hydrogen, ozone, methane, carbon monoxide, helium, neon, krypton and xenon.
bacteria	one-celled organisms visible only through a microscope. Bacteria live all around us and within us.
carbohydrates	these are made up of starchy foods and sugary foods. Starchy foods are very good for us as they give us the best type of energy to help us to work and play all day.
carbon dioxide (CO_2)	colourless, odourless and slightly acidic gas. Carbon dioxide is produced in a variety of ways: by combustion, or oxidation, of materials containing carbon, such as coal, wood, oil or foods; by fermentation of sugars; and by decomposition of carbonates under the influence of heat or acids.

child labour	the full-time employment of children, especially of those who are legally too young to work.
collective bargaining	negotiations between management and a union about pay and conditions of employment on behalf of all the workers in the union.
commodity	a product, merchandise or goods.
consumer	person who buys and uses things.
contaminate	to make something impure, unclean or polluted, especially by mixing harmful impurities into it or by putting it into contact with something harmful.
cultivate	to work land or prepare soil for growing crops.
curriculum	the subjects taught at an educational institution, or the topics taught within a subject.
cyclone	an area of low atmospheric pressure surrounded by a wind system that is blowing in an anti-clockwise direction.
deforestation	indiscriminate cutting or over-harvesting of trees for lumber or pulp, or to clear the land for agriculture, ranching, construction or other human activities. Eighty per cent of the world's original forests have been destroyed.
developing and developed countries	Mainly located in Africa, Asia and Latin America, those nations that are generally less economically advanced than the industrialized nations of the world. Since two-thirds of the world's population are located in these nations they are also known as the Majority World. Where possible it is better to avoid using the phrase 'developing countries'. A better description would be 'the majority world', 'a poor country' or 'countries that are

Glossary

economically poor'. There is a danger that by claiming that we are 'developed countries' while others are 'developing' we claim some kind of misplaced superiority. In many areas we are just as much in need of development as any other country, for example we are now very underdeveloped relationally whereas what we call 'developing' countries are much more developed. Tearfund objects to the definition of 'development' in economic terms only. We should try to be humble and not proclaim our superiority to the rest of the world.

diarrhoea	frequent passage of abnormally watery stools.
diet	the food we eat every day. Diet does not mean a slimming diet that is meant to make people lose weight. There are many diets, but the most important diet is a balanced diet. A balanced diet means we eat the right amount of the right foods.
digestion	this is when the body breaks down the food in our gut (tube that runs from our mouth to our anus, our bottom) to release the nutrients from the food. The body then absorbs the nutrients into the bloodstream, so that the nutrients get taken to parts of the body that need them. The body then gets rid of the waste food (by poohing). This process can take from 12 to 24 hours.
disability	an inability to perform some or all of the tasks of daily life.
Disaster Management Teams:	Tearfund's Disaster Management Team (DMT) has been delivering support and relief to those in areas susceptible to natural disasters for over a decade. Christian partners supported by Tearfund are also helping people living in vulnerable communities to prepare for

	disasters. They strengthen their houses, help them grow more food and discuss what to do in times of emergency.
discrimination	treating people differently.
disease	any harmful change that interferes with the normal appearance, structure or function of the body or any of its parts.
diversifying	to expand into new areas of business, or expand a commercial organization into new areas.
drought	abnormally dry weather within a geographic region where some rain might usually be expected.
ecosystem	organisms living in a particular environment, such as a forest or a coral reef, and the physical parts of the environment that affect them.
emissions	addition of harmful substances to the atmosphere resulting in damage to the environment, human health and quality of life.
energy (food)	the body needs energy to work and play. Energy comes from nutrients in the food that is eaten. The main nutrients that give us energy are carbohydrates, protein and fat. Energy is measured in kilocalories (kcal) or calories (all the same thing).
energy (power)	a source of usable power, such as petroleum or coal.
Ethical Trading Initiative (ETI)	the Ethical Trading Initiative (ETI) is an alliance of companies, non-governmental organizations (NGOs) and trade union organizations. It exists to promote and improve the implementation of corporate codes of practice which cover supply chain working conditions. The ETI's ultimate

Glossary

	goal is to ensure that the working conditions of workers producing for the UK market meet or exceed international labour standards.
excreta	any waste that is passed through the bowels.
Faeces	the body's solid waste matter, composed of undigested food, bacteria, water and bile pigments and discharged from the bowel through the anus.
Fairtrade co-operative	a group of small farmers that, with Fairtrade's help, manage to avoid the middlemen and export their own crops. The members of cooperatives also help each other, lending small sums of money in times of need.
Fairtrade Foundation	the organization responsible for generating greater sales of Fairtrade goods. A registered charity set up by CAFOD, Christian Aid, Oxfam, Traidcraft Exchange and the World Development Movement, it shares internationally recognized Fairtrade standards with initiatives in 18 other countries, working together as Fairtrade Labelling Organisations International (FLO).
Fairtrade Mark	The Fairtrade Mark is an independent consumer label that appears on UK products as a guarantee that they have given their producers a better deal. The mark is awarded by the Fairtrade Foundation.
famine	a severe shortage of food resulting in widespread hunger.
fat	this nutrient gives us the most energy but it is not healthy to have too much fat in our diet. Too much fat makes us become overweight and can also cause your body to get heart disease and other diseases when you get older.

fertilizers an organic or synthetic substance usually added to or spread onto soil to increase its ability to support plant growth.

food aid emergency food assistance in situations of natural and man-made disasters.

Food and Agriculture Organisation the UN agency that leads international efforts to defeat hunger. Serving both developed and developing countries, FAO acts as a neutral forum where all nations meet as equals to negotiate agreements and debate policy. FAO is also a source of knowledge and information. FAO's activities comprise four main areas:
- putting information within reach
- sharing policy expertise
- providing a meeting place for nations
- bringing knowledge to the field.

food security is not just about how much food there is – mathematically speaking, there is enough food in the world for everyone – but people who lack access to it.

fossil fuel energy-rich substances that have formed from long-buried plants and micro-organisms. Fossil fuels, which include petroleum, coal and natural gas, provide most of the energy that powers modern industrial society.

greenhouse effect this happens naturally and is perfectly normal. The atmosphere acts like a massive greenhouse, letting heat in to warm the earth but preventing it from returning into space. It is the enhanced greenhouse effect that is leading to climate change. Carbon dioxide, methane, nitrous oxide and CFCs are the main greenhouse gases responsible. The 'enhanced greenhouse effect' occurs when increased levels of

	these gases are released, causing the blanket to thicken and temperatures to rise to unnaturally high levels. This in turn leads to climate change.
healthy	when your body is fit and well. Healthy also means when something is good for us.
heatwave	a period of unusually hot weather.
HIV	stands for Human Immunodeficiency Virus. The HIV virus infects the cells of the human immune system and begins to destroy or impair their function. It eventually leads to 'immune deficiency', at which point our body is no longer able to fight off infection and disease. Infection with HIV has been established as the underlying cause of AIDS.
house girl	child servants.
hurricane	severe tropical storm with torrential rain and extremely strong winds.
hygiene	the practice or principles of cleanliness.
impunity	exemption from punishment, harm or recrimination.
inhumane	lacking compassion and causing excessive suffering.
International Labour Organisation	this is the UN specialized agency that seeks the promotion of social justice and internationally recognized human and labour rights. The ILO formulates international labour standards in the form of conventions and recommendations, setting minimum standards of basic labour rights: freedom of association, the right to organize, collective bargaining, abolition of forced labour, equality of opportunity and treatment, and other standards regulating conditions across the entire spectrum of work related issues.

irrigation	artificial watering of land to sustain plant growth.
livestock	animals raised for food or other products, or kept for use, especially farm animals such as meat and dairy cattle, pigs and poultry.
living wage	a wage that will allow a worker to support a family in reasonable comfort.
low-income food-deficit countries (LIFDCs)	are currently defined as nations that are: • poor – with a net income per person that falls below the level used by the World Bank to determine eligibility for International Development Association (IDA) assistance. At present, that means that their net income amounts to less than US$1395 per person. • net importers of food – with imports of basic foodstuffs outweighing exports over the past three years. In many cases, particularly in Africa, these countries cannot produce enough food to meet all their needs and lack sufficient foreign exchange to fill the gap by purchasing food on the international market.[87]
malnutrition	a lack of healthy foods in the diet, or an excessive intake of unhealthy foods, leading to physical harm.
minerals	a group of nutrients that the body needs in small quantities to keep it healthy. Some minerals help keep bones and teeth strong. Common minerals are calcium, iron and sodium.
non-govern-active mental organizations (NGOs)	These are non-profit making bodies that are in development work. To qualify for official support, UK non-governmental organizations must be registered charities.[88]
nutrients	the substances that are found in foods that help our bodies to work properly, keep us healthy and give us energy.

nutrition	the study of food and how it affects the health of our bodies.
parasite	a plant or animal that lives on or in another, usually larger, host organism in a way that harms or is of no advantage to the host.
pesticides	chemical substances used to kill pests, especially insects.
pit latrine	a household may choose to dig a shallow unlined pit latrine, which will have a short life, above the water table. When this pit becomes full, the household can simply abandon it and dig a new one.
plantation	a large estate or farm, especially in a hot climate, where crops such as cotton, coffee, tea or rubber trees are grown, usually worked by resident labourers.
pour-flush latrine	the simplest form of pour-flush latrine is the installation of a pan with a water-seal in the defecating hole over a pit.
protein	this nutrient helps us to grow and repairs our bodies.
relief	public help in the form of money, food, clothing, shelter or medicine, provided to people who are temporarily unable to care for themselves.
sanitary protection	sanitary pads and tampons as means of absorbing the blood flow during menstruation.
sanitation	conditions or procedures related to the collection and disposal of sewage and garbage.
septic tank	a tank, usually underground, in which human waste matter is decomposed by bacteria.
sewage	human and domestic waste matter from buildings, especially houses, that is carried away through sewers.

slum	an overcrowded area of a city in which the housing is typically in very bad condition.
special needs	the requirements, especially in education, that some people have because of physical and mental challenges.
staple crop	the basic crop.
starvation	the state of not having enough food, or of losing strength or dying through lack of food.
Sub-Saharan Africa	Sub-Saharan Africa is the term used to describe the 48 nations of Africa that are in or are below the Sahara. In addition to the 42 nations on the African mainland, Sub-Saharan Africa also includes four island nations in the south-west Indian Ocean (Madagascar, The Comoros, Mauritius, and Seychelles) and two island nations in the Atlantic Ocean (Cape Verde and Sao Tome and Principe).
supplementary feeding programme	where enough food is delivered to and consumed by individuals who are in need of an immediate source of nourishment. Supplementary feeding is the most common intervention used by governments of developing countries to improve the nutritional status of small children.
urban drift	people moving from rural areas to the city.
vaccination	a method of stimulating resistance in the human body to specific diseases using micro-organisms – bacteria or viruses – that have been modified or killed. These treated micro-organisms do not cause the disease, but rather trigger the body's immune system to build a defence mechanism that continuously guards against the disease.
vitamins	a group of nutrients needed in small amounts to keep the body healthy. Common vitamins are vitamin A and vitamin C.

Glossary

water-based host   parasites that live in water and carry disease, for example worms.

yield   the amount of something, especially a crop, produced by cultivation or labour.

References

1. Fynn, *Mister God, This is Anna* (London: William Collins, 1974), 27-29
2. WaterAid, www.wateraid.org.uk. A shower uses 5 litres of water a minute; a bath uses 80 litres and flushing the toilet uses 9.5 litres. Luxuries such as a washing machine use 80 litres of water and a dishwasher uses 35 litres. Consumption varies around the world from about 500 litres per person per day in the USA to as little as 20 litres in many developing countries.
3. Thames Water, www.waterinschools.com/watercourse/supply1.htm
4. UNICEF, *A life like mine*: How children live around the world (London: Dorling Kindersley, 2004), 12-13. That's approximately 90 litres (23.5 gallons).
5. Severn Trent Water, www.stwater.co.uk. For every five minutes you're in the shower you use 30 litres (8 gallons) of water.
6. Ibid. For every five minutes you're in a power shower you can use between 75 and 300 litres (20-80 gallons) of water.
7. UNICEF, *A life like mine*, 12-13. That's approximately 5 litres (1.5 gallons).
8. Ibid. That's approximately 10 litres (2.5 gallons).
9. Mid Kent Water, www.midkentwater.co.uk/pdf/aquifer.pdf. That's approximately 7 litres (2 gallons).
10. Ibid. That's approximately 20-30 litres (2.5-5 gallons).
11. UNICEF, *A life like mine*, 12-13. That's approximately 120 litres (31 gallons).
12. World Water Council, *World Water Vision: Making Water Everybody's Business*, 2000
13. Tearfund, *A Tearfund Guide to Water: water in tomorrow's world* (Teddington: Tearfund, 2000), 4
14. Ibid., 8
15. UNICEF, *A life like mine*, 13
16. Make Poverty History, www.makepovertyhistory.org
17. World Health Organization (WHO) and United Nations Children's Fund (UNICEF), Global Water Supply and Sanitation Assessment (2000)
18. Scriptures are quoted from the *International Children's Bible*, New Century Version (Anglicised Edition) copyright 1991 by Authentic Media. Used by permission.
19. Severn Trent Water, www.stwater.co.uk. Every bath you take uses about 110 litres (when filled to a depth of 20 cm), while for every five minutes you're in the shower you use 30 litres of water. Power showers can use between 15 ans 60 litres of water every minute.

[20] Severn Trent Water, www.stwater.co.uk

[21] Institute of Civil Defense and Disaster Studies, www.icdds.org

[22] '*Swept away*', Lifesaver Church Pack, (Teddington: Tearfund, 2002)

[23] *Summary for Policymakers. A Report of Working Group I of the Intergovernmental Panel on Climate Change* (January 2001). On a global scale, three-quarters of the carbon dioxide added to the atmosphere during the last 20 years came from fossil fuel burning and deforestation. Deforestation (cutting down forests to make way for industry) reduces the earth's natural recycling system – plants changing carbon dioxide into oxygen – and disrupts the water cycle, affecting rainfall patterns. According to the New Internationalist (December 1999) an incredible 80 per cent of the world's original forests have so far been destroyed.

[24] Energy Saving Trust. EST is an independent body established by the government to provide free advice to households, businesses and public sector bodies on how to save energy.

[25] *For tomorrow too*: Living responsibly in a world of climate change (Teddington: Tearfund, 2005), 8

[26] Energy Saving Trust

[27] Ibid. You could also try using low energy light bulbs – they use 80 per cent less electricity and last eight to ten times longer than standard bulbs.

[28] Ibid. You could also try turning down your central heating. According to the World Wildlife Fund, just one degree lower can cut ten per cent off fuel bills. Lower the temperature at which you wash your clothes – there is no need to wash clothes above 40°C.

[29] Good Energy (formerly known as unit-e)

[30] Ibid. For more information call Good Energy on 0845 456 1640 (domestic customers) or 0845 456 1650 (business customers), email enquiries@goodenergy.co.uk or visit www.good-energy.co.uk. Quoting UE38 when you make contact will mean a donation to Tearfund.

[31] Energy Saving Trust

[32] Organizations involved in offsetting emissions include Future Forests (www.futureforests.com) and Climate Care (www.climatecare.org). Costs range from about £7 to offset the carbon dioxide emissions from a short flight (e.g. London to Lisbon return), to £15–20 for a return trip to South Africa and £40–50 for a return trip to Australia. For more information on being a responsible tourist visit www.tearfund.org/tourism.

[33] Details of routes near you and free maps can be obtained from Sustrans. call 0117 929 0888 or visit www.sustrans.org.uk.

[34] UK Greenhouse Gas Inventory, 1990 to 2001. Annual Report for Submission under the Framework Convention on Climate Change (July 2003). All landfill sites that contain organic biodegradable material will produce 'landfill gas', which is typically composed of 60 per cent

methane and 40 per cent carbon dioxide, and is normally saturated with moisture. www.wasteonline.org.uk.

35 Rethink Rubbish, www.rethinkrubbish.com. Recycling your organic waste is the most efficient way to reduce the main source of methane emitted by landfill sites.

36 We use around ten billion plastic bags every year in the UK – most of which end up in landfill sites and take 500 years to decompose. To stop junk mail register at the Mailing Preference Service at www.mpsonline.org.uk or call 020 7291 3310.

37 You can find out where your nearest recycle banks for non-organic waste are by visiting www.recycle-more.co.uk or calling Recycle-More on 08450 682 572. Your local council may offer a kerbside recycling service.

38 *International Children's Bible*

39 *International Children's Bible*

40 *Summary for Policymakers*

41 UN Food and Agriculture Organisation, Food Security Assessment 1996.

42 *Biteback* (Teddington: Tearfund, 2002), 13

43 Ibid.

44 *A Tearfund guide to food security: bridging the gap* (Teddington: Tearfund, 2001), 5

45 Ibid.

46 Christian Aid, www.christian-aid.org.uk

47 *International Children's Bible*

48 UN Food and Agriculture Organisation, Food Security Assessment 1996.

49 The Independent, 'What a waste: Britain's bulging bin bags' (Friday 15 April 2005), based on research by the United Nations and the Catholic aid organization (CAFOD).

50 Ibid.

51 It has been suggested that the European Union is proposing to ban the disposal of food in landfill sites from January 2006 onwards.

52 ILO Report 2000

53 Ibid.

54 Clean Clothes Campaign

55 Labour behind the Label, Wearing Thin report (2001)

56 Mark Curtis, *Trade for Life: making trade work for poor people*, (London: Christian Aid, 2001)

57 National Labour Committee.

58 Labour behind the Label

59 CAFOD, *Fashion Victims: the Asian garment industry and globalisation*, November 1998

60 *International Children's Bible*

61 Ethical Trading Initiative (ETI). This means that there should be no forced or prison labour. Workers should be free to leave their employer after a period of notice.

62 Ethical Trading Initiative (ETI). This basically means that workers should be able to join or form trade unions of their own choosing and be able to bargain for better wages and working conditions. Workers' union reps should not be treated badly in the workplace and should be free to carry out whatever duties they have.

63 Ethical Trading Initiative (ETI). This means that, amongst other things, steps should be taken to prevent accidents and injuries in the workplace. Workers should have regular health and safety training and access to clean toilets. Workers' accommodation should be clean and safe.

64 Ethical Trading Initiative (ETI). This means that no children (anyone under the age of 15 qualifies as a child unless the local law in the country says a higher or lower age for work or schooling) should be recruited, and that if children are found to be working in the company a programme should be set up to enable that child to attend quality education until they are no longer a child. Child labour means work that is done by children younger than the age above, which is likely to be dangerous or to interfere with the child's education.

65 Ethical Trading Initiative (ETI). Excessive hours means working more than 48 hours a week on a regular basis and not having one day off for every seven days worked. No one should be forced to do overtime or expected to do it on a regular basis, but if they choose to do it they should not have to do more than 12 hours per week and they should be paid well for it.

66 Ethical Trading Initiative (ETI). Discrimination means being treated differently to others because of factors like race, religion, age, disability, gender, marital status, being a member of a trade union or your political beliefs. When workers are chosen for recruitment, training or promotion, everyone should be treated equally.

67 Ethical Trading Initiative (ETI). This means that there should be legal contracts written up when any work is to be carried out - so that people can not be insecure in their work, knowing how long they can expect to work for and under what agreement. No harsh or inhumane treatment is allowed.

68 Ethical Trading Initiative (ETI). This means that workers should not be abused verbally, physically or sexually – or intimidated or threatened in any other way.

69 Ethical Trading Initiative (ETI). A living wage is a wage that should be enough to meet workers' basic needs such as food, healthcare, education and accommodation. Often a living wage is higher than a country's minimum wage.
70 London Fashion Week Report (2004)
71 David Ransom, *No Nonsense Guide to Fair Trade* (London: Verso Books, 2001)
72 World (FAO, 2002). www.uga.edu/fruit/banana.htm. Top ten Countries (% of world production) are: India (24%), Ecuador (9%), Brazil (9%), Philippines (8%), China (8%), Indonesia (5%), Costa Rica (3%), Mexico (3%), Thailand (2%), Colombia (2%)
73 The Sugar Bureau, www.sugar-bureau.org
74 Fairtrade Foundation, www.fairtrade.org.uk
75 Fairtrade Foundation. The 'Unpeeling the Banana Trade' report in 2002 revealed that the UK spends about £750 million on bananas each year.
76 Ibid.
77 British Coffee Association: Men drink 1.7 cups a day and women 1.5.
78 Fairtrade Foundation. The minimum Fairtrade price for a kilogram of the arabica coffee bean is about £1.80 and for the robusta its £1.50. In February 2002 this was 168% and 468% above the respective international market price.
79 Ibid.
80 Ibid.
81 Download a full list of products at www.fairtrade.org.uk/downloads/pdf/fairtrade_products.pdf.
82 *International Children's Bible*
83 *International Children's Bible*
84 'Missing the Mark: A 'School Report' on rich countries' contribution to Universal Primary Education by 2015' (Global Campaign for Education, 2005). www.oxfam.org.uk/what_we_do/issues/education/gce_missing.htm
85 Jubilee Debt Campaign, www.jubileedebtcampaign.org.uk
86 UNICEF, *A life like mine*, 48.
87 Food and Agriculture Organisation, www.fao.org
88 DFID, www.dfid.gov.uk